And... I Met Myself

KETAN KARINGWAR

Copyright © 2024 by Ketan Karingwar

All rights reserved.

This book or any portion thereof may not be reproduced or used in any manner whatsoever without the express written permission of the respective writer of the respective content except for the use of brief quotations in a book review.

The writer of the respective work holds sole responsibility for the originality of the content and The Write Order is not responsible in any way whatsoever.

Printed in India

ISBN: 978-93-6045-456-2

First Printing, 2024

The Write Order
A division of Nasadiya Technologies Private Ltd.
Koramangala, Bengaluru
Karnataka-560029

THE WRITE ORDER PUBLICATIONS.

www.thewriteorder.com

Edited by Ridham Bassi

Typeset by MAP Systems, Bengaluru

Book Cover designed by Sankhasubhro Nath

Publishing Consultant - Samyuktha Prasanan

With heartfelt gratitude, this dedication is lovingly made to my parents. They brought me into this beautiful world, laying the foundation for my existence. Today, as I experience the wonders of God's creation – The Universe, I am filled with appreciation and joy.

Acknowledgment

I would like to thank my wife–Rohini–for pushing me into publishing this book, which was never part of my plans. This journey began in 2010, and finally, it will see bookshelves in 2024.

Immense gratitude for my brother, Chetan, for being the best brother and a wonderful family man. His wife, Priti, for being the epitome of simplicity and light-heartedness, and finally, my sister, Bhavana.

Special thanks to all my friends– Sandeep, Sachin, Ashish, Jayant, Amol, Amit, Vishal, Ram, Mohan, Swati, Dipti, Rakhi, and Sneha– for being there no matter what. I certainly may have missed a few names, but you all are equally important and part of the journey I have penned down.

Thank you, dear reader, for picking this book up and giving it a fair chance. I genuinely hope this story finds a place in your hearts.

I wouldn't want to leave out the efforts of The Write Order team. Ms. Samyuktha Prasanan, the Publishing Consultant, for being proactively responsive, professional and at the same time so kind throughout the entire process. Ms. Ridham Bassi, the Editor, for helping me refine the language and breathing life into my efforts. This book is the combined effort of all our toiling, thank you, team.

And of course, last but above all, God. For paving this way for me to walk on.

Preface

This book is about the story of a typical lower middle-class Indian boy, Akhil, who one day, on his way to work, sees a few youngsters discussing certain things. He becomes more attentive to the conversation being held amongst those youngsters whereby he understands that one of the persons from that group has just passed engineering and is about to join his first job, whom he calls 'Center Boy'. Akhil then reaches his office; however, he is moved by the episode he just witnessed. He relates himself to the 'Centre Boy' and feels as if the 'Centre Boy' is none other but himself. He then thinks of traveling back in time and revisiting each moment he has spent till then, in his life. And thus through this book he tells us about the journey of his life.

This Volume-I covers his journey until he is admitted to his professional studies, i.e., engineering. In this entire journey, he recalls every moment he spent, the ups and downs he had, and the joys and sorrows he experienced. This book covers the innocence of a child, the warmth he feels when he is with his parents, and invaluable lessons learnt from his parents, specifically his mother. Also covered is his one-sided liking for a girl whom he calls 'Childhood Crush,' who happens to be the daughter of the trustee of the school where he studied till the seventh grade. It captures the innocence and beauty of that feeling when he talks about the childhood crush. Importantly, it has nothing to do with matters of sex, bonding, emotions, or being together.

And how that girl turns out to be the reason for his exit from the school. It also tells us that the world is a small place, making us strongly believe in the power of the almighty, what we call a miracle.

Disclaimer

This is a work of fiction. Unless otherwise indicated, all the names, characters, businesses, places, events and incidents in this book are either the product of the author's imagination or used in a fictitious manner. Any resemblance to actual persons, living or dead, or actual events is purely coincidental.

"Mere Desh Ki Dharti Sona Ughle, Ughle Hire Moti, Mere Desh Ki Dharti ..."

It was August 15th, 2010; I was waiting for my company bus, in front of the Navbharat Press, to attend my "B" shift duty, and the lyrics were making me whisper the song that is one of my favorites, as it was being played at a nearby kiosk. Hold on, you might think, August 15th and office? Wait, I will answer this question later.

"Arey yaar, Rahul ka kya hua?" (What about Rahul?) *"Pata nahi yaar"* (I Don't know) *"Aur haan Sakshi, wo kya kehti hai?"* (And yes, what does Sakshi say?). *"Arey uski to shadi hai agle mahine."* (She is getting married next month). *"Yaar, ye ladkiyo ka mast hai, shadi karo tension free."* (One thing is good with girls, they can get married, be happy with no tension.)

Some discussion at my back was making me attentive towards listening to it, though I wasn't that interested in it, but to satisfy the senses, I got a bit attentive towards it and turned around to get the know-how of what it was and I could see a group of four to five young Indians quenched in discussing the all-important matter. On becoming more attentive to it, I could crack; the boys had just passed engineering, and one of them was selected by a prime cement manufacturing company located in Chandrapur, some 160-170 Km from Nagpur. I could easily see the eyes of the center boy—the one who was selected in a campus interview—full of dreams, future plans, and what not. Suddenly, a private travel bus arrived, and the boy started making his way to it.

"Kalji ghe... khyal rakhana" (Take care, bye...), keep calling, and keep mailing were some of the usual words knocking on my eardrums as the boy got closer to the bus. Turning my head a few degrees, I could see the mom and sister of the Center Boy with their teary eyes. It hardly took anything for me to understand that those were nothing but 'happy tears', or the so-called *'khushi ke aansoo'*, and the dear father

was waving his hands to convey his love to the dear son, but the limitless love that he had in his heart for the dear son was being revealed anyway.

The bus started to pick up, and in a few minutes, I could only see the lines, *"Aii chi punyayi"*—*"Maa ki dua"*—*"Blessing of Mother"*—written on the back of the bus which too disappeared after some time. After the departure of the center boy, everybody came to know that they had to get back, and with heavy hearts, they put on a back gear and, in some time, went off.

"Sala bus nahi ayi abhi tak?" ('Fuck, man! The bus has still not arrived!') no, I wasn't cursing anybody, but just whispering these words to myself in frustration. I have been a gentleman ever since I was born, no question of abusing others. In a moment, the light flickered and I came to know it was 15th of August! The commotion and the noise of traffic, horns, and whistles weren't like the usual. Those fast moving cars, that heavy traffic, those clouds of carbon monoxide coming out of the silencers were not as much as they would usually be. It was quite a calm noon, as almost everybody had enjoyed the morning and was probably resting at home at noon. Those with extra energy were enjoying it at the destined places; hence, the roads were breathing a bit freely at noon.

My mind again got back to the episode I saw a few minutes ago, and I was now totally into it. Where will the Centre Boy go? How much will he earn? Will he be able to stay away from his home? Will he be happy with the first job he lands? So many questions started playing all the musical instruments in my mind, creating a complete cacophony. I just shook my head to shrug all of those questions from my mind and closed my eyes to regain my composure.

"Sir, chalo, kya hua?" (Sir, what happened? Let's go.) Our bus conductor asked me as the bus had come, and I was standing still, with my eyes

closed. Hearing this voice from nowhere, I got back to life from my short space round and made my way into the bus.

"*Musafir hu yaro...Na ghar hai na thikana,*" yes, I, being a diehard fan of old songs, specifically those of Kishor Kumar, took no time to get sunk into the song being played in the bus. The bus took off for the company, some 35-40 km from Nagpur, and I went in the lap of a queen... '*Nidra Rani*', yes, I went into a deep slumber in no time. "*Sir, uthiye,*" (Sir, please get up) the bus conductor yelled as we were now at the factory door. I got up and made my way in. After putting in-punch, I started to make my way to the shop floor but could hardly see a gathering of 8-10 workers, which otherwise remained in masses, for the same reason—August 15th.

I got into the shop and took charge of the shift. But small crackers of joy had already started to burst in my mind, as I had already sensed a few workers. August 15th meant no load, no heavy work, or planning for the shift... Get back to the cabin and pass your time by reading or doing something else you find interesting.

I planned the shift and got back to the cabin. I took my bag to get a pen, which was there in a pouch, and saw a book in my bag, which my brother had been insisting I read for the last 3–4 days—the famous one by Chetan Bhagat "Two States." I pulled it out of the bag and started to read.

After finishing off the hundred and sixty pages, though the book was too interesting, I started to feel a bit uneasy. I put the book aside and closed my eyes for a moment, but I could not resist one thing: the thoughts about 'Centre Boy'. Yes, he was still there in mind, and I decided to get back to him. I started to think about him once again, and then I could crack the perplexity of why the 'Centre Boy' was troubling me. Actually, he wanted me to meet someone. He wanted me to meet me.

And... I Met Myself

And it was on August 15th, 2010 that I met myself.

I decided to meet every moment, every stage, and every form Akhil had spent, and hence started with child Akhil. I closed my eyes and went into the past. Retrospecting, I went as far back as I could.

"Sharda Bhavan," a primary school in Nanded, is where we three—my brother, sister, and I—were in my sister's class, and she was opening the tiffin as it was a lunch break. She served us like a mother does. We three started to take the efforts made by Mom to cook the tiffin to their final destination by finishing off the tiffin. "Tan Tan Tan," the bell rang to indicate that the recess was over. Both of us—my brother and I—went to our classes.

At 2:30 pm, the time every child used to wait for, rang the final bell, giving us the freedom to move out of the school, and almost everyone started to run as if an animal from a zoo were being kept in a cage for more than a year or so.

In Nanded, we used to live in a rented house, and we had no relatives except a paternal aunt. She had a daughter and two sons. Because there were only two families there to get to know each other, as almost all of our relatives stayed in Nagpur, we two used to stay nearer each other. The general routine used to be that the 'fathers' from both families would go to work, the 'mothers' of the houses, for some shopping or so, and we six used to be at home. I can still recall the days when we would play together and both the sisters—my sister and my aunt's daughter—would take care of us like mothers do.

I could not gather too many memories of Nanded, as we had not spent too much time but only 2 years, or, in other words, I was unable to collect all the memories. The only things I could clearly recall were a few days spent together playing as children, a Gurudwara—the famous one of Nanded after the Golden Temple, as we used to stay nearby—and a flooded day when Godavari, one of the prime rivers of India, got completely violent.

All in all, Nanded wasn't in a prominent memory as I was a child at the time and only studied for the first two grades there, or even less—half term of the second grade. One thing I forgot to mention is that my father had a job that had him transferred to various locations within Maharashtra, which meant I attended school in multiple places, around three or four different ones.

My Hero, Moving To Warthi, A Small Village In Bhandara District

Yes, my father is my biggest hero for all his hard work and the kind of innocent and human character he has. To tell you a little about him, my grandfather had eight offsprings who survived. Yes, he almost built up a cricket team with reserved players as well, but poverty didn't let him manage all of them until their survivable growth.

There were four daughters and four sons who survived. Destiny cannot always be harsh with you, and it was revealed when it allowed Dadaji, my grandfather, to maintain equilibrium here with four sons and four daughters.

My father, being fourth after two sisters, a brother, and the second elder of the brothers, had a lot of responsibilities. Yes, the situation was more or less similar to an old Hindi movie, but again, it was a fact. My father used to go on daily wages to earn some bread and butter and would study under a street lamp at night. He was very good at his studies and wanted to be a lawyer, but unfortunately, it could not happen.

After completing his pre-education (some ten plus two at that time), he got a government job, and with his first salary, he bought an electricity connection at home, thus bringing that much-needed light, which now had become the basic need after the sunset. Yes, he really brought light to the family in many ways.

And thereafter, there are too many things to be covered in a book that made him a hero in my eyes. Yes, he is my hero.

So after Nanded, the next destination was Warthi. My father was quite happy, as after staying away from home for almost 11-12 years, he was moving closer to his home, his family, and Warthi, which is some 70–80 km from Nagpur. In the span of 11-12 years, he had been to Chandrapur, Gadchiroli (a Naxalite area of Maharashtra), and Nanded.

Then came the day to leave Nanded. With a heavy heart, Mom hugged Aunt, as now Aunt's was the only family left there in Nanded. Tears started rolling down their eyes. I could not understand why just a slight detachment was making them cry as if they were separating, never to meet again. Initially, the whole drama was a bit fun for me, but as we started to walk away from them—Aunty and the family—my heart too got a bit heavy. It was hard for me to understand what had suddenly happened to me, but something was amiss.

I felt as if I was missing out on something in life that probably would never come back.

I looked at my brothers and sisters, my own, and my aunt's daughter and son; their eyes were also wet, and all of us now understood that we were going to miss those precious moments we had spent together—that love, that quarreling, the fun we had in each other's company, that *masti (fun)*, everything.

Here, I understood what role the heart plays in one's body. I was trying to conceal my tears, but I couldn't. The truth was, the time we spent together was never going to come back. In fact, there was no going back to Nanded for us as we left.

We All Moved From Nanded To Warthi, Leaving All Those Memories Behind

'Oh God, where have I landed?'

Yes, that was the question I had in mind when we landed there in Warthi, a relatively small town in Bhandara district when compared to Nanded, where we had spent the past couple of years.

Of course, I can still recall the place where we used to stay in Warthi. It was a place that was very close to nature, and I used to feel as if we were completely in the lap of nature. A typical drawing book picture was what that place was. A complete lush green field around with too many shrubs, a small hill, and a lake—a completely out-of-the-world place for the little kid that I was.

A few memories that I have from Warthi... a weekly market that used to be on Thursday; now I recall this clearly because it used to be a half day for the school as our school was amidst the market. School! Hold on... Let me tell you about my school there in Warthi. I have a mild smile when I am narrating this. And yes, how can I not talk about my very first day at the school there in Warthi? So let me start with my attire on the very first day: a white Kurta, a white dhoti—of course, a dhoti with elastic adjustment at the waist—needless to mention, I was a kid going to the third grade, so a dhoti with elastic adjustment, and a Gandhi topi (cap).

And this is where I yelled those words: 'Oh God, where have I landed?'

I mean, from half pants and a shirt to attire like this one, it was making me so uncomfortable. I was so annoyed with my hero—my dad—thinking about why he got me admitted to such a school. Aren't there good schools here where we have a similar dress code that we have been putting on for the last two years or so? But it was very difficult for a child like me to understand that it was a very small place where only a couple of schools, which I was basically thinking about, were available. And with the responsibility of raising all three of us equally and the kind of economic condition we had, my father could have never afforded all three of us to get admitted to those schools.

One thing to mention precisely is that every single parent wants to give the best to their child, but they also have to be practical enough at the same time. They burn the candle at both ends to give the best to their offspring; what else do they not do to raise their blood? But, alas, the questions we, as their children, ask them when we grow up are: *Kya kiya aap logo ne mere liye?* (What have you done for me?), *Acha school or college nhi de sakte to paida kyo kiya?* (If you can't get us admitted to a good school or college, then why did you give birth to us?). To all those children, my submission is: You will also be a parent tomorrow; pray to the almighty that the questions don't bounce back to you.

Think for a while about what parents feel when their children ask these never-expected or never-anticipated, heartbreaking questions. Those who have been reading this right now and have behaved like this when they were children might feel bad for their behavior. Anyway, that time has gone, and they are your parents, so though they may not have forgotten that incident, those questions, or that moment, surely they might have forgiven you for that act. Please go and say sorry right now. But for those who have lost their parents and are experiencing heavy hearts for that kind of behavior while reading this, they can only say sorry to the unknown. Anyway, please get your composure back.

My submission here to those who are about to do this is: please don't ever hurt your parents by asking such worthless questions, because you will only know what your parents did for you once you are a parent. But please wait until that time and don't jump to these questions before that.

Anyway, *bahot senti ho gaya* (I got too emotional).

Now let's get your composure back and move on to my story.

Yes, so... with that attire, I went to school—the first day of school. I am unable to recall who took me to school—Dad or Mom—all I can recall is a small, half-built, rough-constructed room with cotton strips laid to sit on.

One more thing I want to mention here is that a lot of things have already gone into oblivion while I write this, but a few small, rough memories that I have like: There was a rail track adjacent to the school, and whenever a train used to pass by, the entire room, or school, would shake, leaving me in a complete panic about whether the room would collapse.

So, back to my first day as I entered the class, I was new to all of them, and vice versa... everyone started staring at me, and so was I at everyone. Anyhow, I managed to sit on the mat laid on the floor.

And, needless to mention, I sat at the extreme end of the row.

"Gajanan..."

"Ho, Guruji..."

"Suresh..."

"Aho, Guruji..."

"Pankaj..."

"Hazar, Guruji..."

All were affirming their presence in the school as our teacher was marking the attendance.

"Akhil..."

"Yes, Sir."

"Ha ha ha!" The entire classroom erupted into laughter as I yelled "Yes, sir," leaving me completely shattered, isolated, and alone. I was just looking here and there with so many questions in my mind. *Maine kya bol diya?* (What did I say?), *Koi galti kar di kya?* (Did I make any mistake?)—So many questions started troubling me, and the class was still laughing. Finally, to help me, came our class teacher, who asked the entire class to keep quiet and came to me.

Moving his hand over my head, he said, *"Beta… 'ho guruji,' 'sir' nahi"* (Child, it's 'ho guruji', and not 'sir'). And let me tell you very openly: I was not getting what exactly was happening there.

All I could understand was the feeling of being a small kid left on his own who had traveled from a relatively urban location like Nanded to a more typical rural area like Warthi. Let me tell you the truth: I was literally crying as all those students were still laughing at me.

Anyway, the year-long day—the first day of school—finally ended, and I could see my mom waiting for me outside the school. I was so delighted to see a known face, which was hard for the past few hours of school, and that too, Mom, that my joys knew no boundaries the moment I saw her.

Without wasting a single minute, I ran to her and clutched her as if I were not going to leave her ever. And of course, needless to mention, I started crying.

"Kay zal?" (What happened?), *"Arey ka radtos kay zal tula?"* (Hey, what happened? Why are you crying?)

Mom tried to calm me.

"Mi nahi yenar hya shalet," (I won't come to this school), *"Mala nahi avdli hi shala,"* (I didn't like this school), *"Mala sarv hastat."* (Everyone laughs at me).

I started complaining to her about the school. *"Mi tuzyasobat gharich rahil."* (I will stay at home with you).

I was just uttering sentences one after the other, and she was making all her efforts to calm me down.

Eventually, being a mother, she managed to calm me down, and we two left for home. That evening, I was desperately waiting for my father to come back home from the office, as I was eager to narrate to him the entire episode of the first day that I had spent in school.

When he came back around seven in the evening, I ran to him, and without letting him even have a glass of water, let alone a cup of tea, I started to narrate to him the entire drama.

One thing I specifically want to mention here is that my dad was so tired that day, as it was a new place for him as well. He had to cope with the work environment, people, workload, etc., so probably he was in no mood to listen to my day's drama narration. But I only came to know this today while I was writing it. That day, as I already said above, I didn't even let him breathe and started telling the day's story, and like every father does, he was all happy, carefully listening to what his child was telling him.

"Mi janar nahi mhanje nahi tya shulet," (I won't go to that school) were the words that finally concluded my story. And he said, *"Thik ahe, nako jaus udyapasn."* (Ok, stop going there from tomorrow).

I was so delighted to hear those words from him that I quickly left him and went to the kitchen to tell Mom that Dad had approved of not going to school the next day. She too gave me a mild smile and said, "Okay, no issues; don't go; happy?" And really, I was so happy that I can't narrate my ecstasy here. But for the small kid that I was, the joy only lasted for that night, as the next morning both came to me and started convincing me to go to school. They were bribing me with chocolates, toys, and new clothes, but I was very firm about not going to school. But eventually, I fell short in front of their power and started walking towards school with my father.

But today I had a plan in mind to get back home within an hour. As my father dropped me off at school and saw me off, I started to think about executing my plan. After an hour or so, I went to the class teacher and said, *"Guruji aaj amchyakade Satya Narayan Puja ahe, mhanun mala lavkar ghari jayala lagel."* (Sir, we have Satya Narayan Pooja at our home, so I need to go home early).

I was quite skeptical about whether that plan would work or not, but to my surprise, it took no time for the teacher to give his approval.

"Okay, go," he said.

After an hour and a half, I took my bag and started walking back—yes, alone. I was very scared about whether I would reach home safely. What would my parents say when they learned that I had come alone? With so many questions in my mind, I finally reached home safely.

I saw my mom with a few ladies in the front yard; she quickly came to me and asked, "What happened? Why did you come home so early, and with whom have you come back?"

I was in no mood to answer any of her questions. I made my way into the house and started crying. She followed me into the home, came to me, and asked, "What happened?"

Finally, with a lot of courage, I told her about the entire incident. She was all smiles, but at the same time, she showed me that she was too angry with me. I could clearly see a mom's confusion about whether to scold the child for the act he did or pamper him for the kind of phase he was going through, and yes, of course, how he planned and came back home. There is a mild smile on my face while I narrate this.

This lasted for a few days—my drama of not going to school. I forgot to mention one thing here: my brother and sister were in the same school and would happily go to school right from the first day.

Eventually, I too started going to school regularly. And that's how we started living in Warthi.

Nagpur Calling, Year: 1990-1991

Warthi just turned out to be a sojourn, where we stayed only for eight to nine months or so. The Almighty had a very different plan for my parents. My father suffered some sort of illness that was not being properly diagnosed. He started losing his weight drastically. He would come home from the office and stay calm. We were not seeing the father we saw in the past few years. He used to stay within himself. However, we were too young to understand the difficulties and health issues he was facing and the bad patch our parents were going through. All I can recall is that Dad traveled a few times to Nagpur to see good doctors there.

Today I can recall those few words that my parents would discuss between them about getting relocated to Nagpur, as we were the only family there in Warthi with no relatives around. And with Papa's health issues, both of them wanted to get back to Nagpur; as I already told you, almost all of our relatives would stay in Nagpur.

One thing I want to specifically tell you here is that it's August 29th, 2010, at 2 a.m. in the morning when I am writing this, and it's basically Sunday, and I am in the middle of my night shift. It's a short break for snacks and tea, and all my colleagues are there in the canteen for that. Before I put what's in my mind, which is about to come on paper, my eyes are wet.

The reason for this, as I mentioned earlier, was that this was the period when my father's health started deteriorating. My mother, a remarkable and strong woman, took care of all of us with immense dedication. During that time, my father was preoccupied with his work, health issues, and the stress of providing for the family, but he was also deeply grateful for the support he received from his life partner. I have the utmost respect and admiration for my mom.

She might scold, yell, and sometimes be strict, but she also showers us with love, care, and affection. 'Thank you, God, for the wonderful parents you've given me,' I often think. I couldn't have asked for better parents than the ones I have today.

"Abe kya kar raha?" (Hey man, what are you doing?) My colleagues asked me, as they were now in the office with the snacks and the tea.

"Abe ro raha hai kya?" (Hey, are you crying?) asked one of the colleagues who was a bit closer to me.

"Nahi be, just aankh mein kuch gaya hai," (No, I am alright; there is some dust in my eyes; I am absolutely fine) I replied.

"Ok, let's go back to the shop floor; the shift has resumed," my colleague said.

"Okay," I said, nodding my head in agreement. And we went to the shop floor.

Of course, with a heavy heart and numb eyes, as I was still down the memory lane in my mind, recalling all those days and missing my parents badly.

And finally arrived the day when, one day my father came back home and told my mom, "Zali transfer." (I am transferred to Nagpur.)

I could tell he was not exactly ecstatic about the transfer order because he's someone who can perform well even in challenging situations, but he did feel at ease with the idea of relocating to Nagpur. It was because he was going back to his hometown, reuniting with his family and friends. So, yes, to some extent, he was happy that day. Eventually, a few days later, we packed up and moved to Nagpur. As described earlier, our time in Warthi turned out to be a brief stopover, lasting only eight to nine months.

And thus we moved to Nagpur

- The memories I hold dear from my time in Warthi are vivid and etched in my mind. It was a place enveloped in lush greenery, with a serene lake close by. The weekly Thursday market was a unique experience, making it a half-day at school. I remember my school, my classmates, and that unforgettable first day at school, full of excitement and anticipation. And then, there was a song, "Ude Jab Jab Zulfe Teri...," a tune that our landlord often played on lazy afternoons, and I cherished listening to it. Warthi was a chapter in my life filled with these simple yet precious moments that I carry with me.

So, somewhere in March–April 1991, we eventually came to Nagpur. While writing this, I could recall that my father was so delighted now that he was with his family, as by that time he had spent almost 12–13 years away from a heavily crowded joint family. One can imagine how hard it was for both of my parents to stay away from home at that age, when the means of communication and transportation were not that developed. Yes, of course, a lot of families have done that. How would both of them have managed all this during that time? They, too, surely might have gone through thick and thin during the time they spent away from the family.

And yes, how they would have felt when they lost their daughter in that hustle of life, traveling from one place to another. This part I didn't touch until now. I lost one of my sisters, who was older than me, when she was probably four or five years of age. I don't remember too much of her except her name, 'Sakshi'.

My father had been to Kurudwadi (a place near Pandharpur), Chandrapur, Nanded, Warthi, and then Nagpur in the span of 12–13 years of his service. And I was born in Chandrapur in 1983. All these years, ever since we grew up, until today, we only heard of

Sakshi from our parents and elderly people or relatives. All agree that she was very beautiful and good-looking compared to the three of us siblings. One thing to mention is that she died just a few days after her birthday. The day she died, she had put on the same dress Papa had bought her on her birthday. Since then, there have been no birthday celebrations at our home. In fact, all through these years, birthdays have never been a special event at our home. We never celebrated the birthdays of any of the five of us all through these years. Anyway, I don't want to write too much about the sister I lost for two reasons. One is that I truly don't remember much of her—not even a single moment shared. On the other hand, I don't want you to get into unnecessary sentiments and emotions.

Finally, as I told you above, somewhere in March–April 1991, we came to Nagpur.

Now, let me tell you about my Nagpur family. It was a joint family of almost 18–19 people who would stay in a 275-square-foot house. Yes, of course, there used to be some noises around. When those many people live together, it's bound to happen, but having said that, we used to live in complete harmony with one kitchen, precisely for all those 18–19 people. When I say 18–19 people, 17 were the permanent members, and a couple of guys would stay on and off. They were the cousins of my father, and yes, they were still unmarried in their 40s.

So one can imagine how a family of 18–19 members would stay in a 275-square-foot home. Of course we were an economically backward class (not mentioning this to tell anyone, but the fact, well, leave it), but the kind of bonding we had, for that matter, was there amongst three brothers, as one of my uncles would stay in Mumbai, and he still stays in Mumbai, was exemplary. So, the three brothers, i.e., my father and his elder and younger brother, their families, and their parents, i.e., my grandparents, so we started living happily in

Nagpur, completely enjoying those moments, which I will probably never forget for the rest of my life.

However, it didn't last too long; my grandmother, who was suffering from leukaemia, died on June 17, 1991. I can still recall that Monday, though I was a kid at the time. I remember a few moments spent with my grandmother. She was a very strict lady who would love to live her life with great discipline. I could only spend a few months with her as we had just moved to Nagpur. We used to come to Nagpur on summer vacations or Diwali vacations for the last three years or so, which we had spent in Nanded and Warthi, but no moments are there in the prominent memory of the time I spent with my grandmother. I can only recollect her face as I retrospect those days.

Anyway for a child, all that was happening that Monday was very casual, as I was yet to be trapped in the net of emotions of relation, affinity, love, bonding, family, and all.

School Life In Nagpur

After having studied at two different places, i.e., Nanded and Warthi, now it was time for me to go to school in the third place, i.e., Nagpur. I was so confused and unconvinced that this would be a comparatively better place. I thought of again putting on a Dhoti, Kurta, and Topi as the school uniform and started asking my parents not to get me admitted to any such school where I would again have to put on that dress code. I was in all my efforts convincing them that the uniform I had in my previous school didn't suit me at all, and I was so uncomfortable with it. And, of course, the fear of a train track passing adjacent to the school was always there. However, what both of my parents would give me was a mild smile at my grievance.

Having had all the negotiations with my parents, which I feel was worthless, because anyway, I got admitted to the pre-decided school where all of my cousins were studying, and for that matter, where even my father and uncle studied, I finally landed in the school. Unlike today, there were no English-medium schools; for that matter, we knew not, or the reach wasn't there, where my parents could afford me to study.

It was typically a Marathi-medium school where I, along with my brother and sister, finally got admitted. So all in all, we were eight-nine cousins studying at the same school.

Thus started my school life in Nagpur. I was in fourth grade. Getting down to the memory lane in the school I am trying to remember as much as I can. The school had two buildings, or premises, separated by a road. The first one used to be for classes from 1 to 4, while the other would house classes from 5 to 10.

My first day at school, as I mentioned earlier, was a day filled with uncertainties, particularly concerning the school uniform and the train tracks. As my father and I travelled to school, I kept hoping that I wouldn't have to wear that uniform, follow that dress code, and, of course, deal with those train tracks.

Speaking of the doubts that can swirl in a child's mind, I was already dressed in a 'Khaki' uniform, which was a light olive green color, with a half pant and a white shirt. Yet, I was still uncertain if I would be wearing the same uniform at this new school. With my mind all muddled with these thoughts, we finally arrived at the school.

And what I saw there at a very first glance, I just jerked away my hand and freed myself from my father and tried to run away.

"Arey beta, thamb kay zal?" (Hey child, stop, what happened?), shouted my father, who followed me. Being a kid, it took no time for him to get hold of me back.

"Kay zal?" (What happened?) This time it was more of a father asking his confused, scared son. "Papa," I said while pointing my finger at the man who was conducting the class.

At this instance, we were at the gate of the school, and for the fourth standard I was going to attend, the classroom was such that the teacher could be seen from the very gate of the school while the students would sit back to the door. Of course, I only came to know later that this is the fourth standard classroom. And that I would be sitting in the same room.

Returning to that moment, I turned to my father and pointed at the man who seemed to be the class teacher. He was dressed in an outfit I had a strong aversion to – a 'DHOTI,' a 'KURTA,' and a 'GANDHIAN TOPI.' I cannot express enough how displeased I was with my father at that point. In that instant, memories of my first day at my previous school came flooding back, and I began to cry, saying, *"Mi ithe nahi shiknar"* (I won't study here). I implored my father repeatedly, "Please, take me home. I just don't want to stay here." My father, baffled, asked, *"Arey, pan kay zal? Ka nahi ithe shikayach?"* (What happened? Why don't you want to study here?). I continued to cry, saying, *"Papa, dhoti kurta...mi sangitl na tumhala."* (Dad, I already told you...see, the same dress code is here).

My father attempted to soothe my anxiety and said, "Hey, look, it's the attire of the class teacher, not the students. Just observe." He said, "See all the students over there; they are wearing regular uniforms." With a reassuring gesture, he wiped away my tears and continued, "So, don't worry. You won't have to wear a dhoti and kurta. What you're wearing right now is your uniform."

His words put me at ease, and I regained my composure, glancing at the class and smiling at my father. I exclaimed, *"Kharach na, Papa?"* (Really, Dad? Are you sure?).

He affirmed, "Ho re, bala" (Yes, my child). Finally, I breathed a sigh of relief and thanked God for hearing the prayers I had been silently uttering on the way to school.

And I got admitted to that school, thus starting my school life in Nagpur; needless to mention, my sister and my brother were also admitted to the same school. My sister, being in sixth grade, would go to the other building, while my brother and I would go to the comparatively smaller campus, which, as I already said, would house the classes until fourth grade, only starting from the first grade.

Childhood Crush

Hold on for a moment. I can see the gentle smiles on your faces as you read this heading, but let me clarify something. I'm not writing a love story, mine or anyone else's. In fact, I'm not even certain what I'm writing or for whom. I'm not sure if what I'm putting down on paper will ever reach anyone. This is more of a personal introspection.

Who am I? What am I? What have I accomplished up to this point, and what will I do in the future? To be completely honest, I'm just reflecting on these questions and jotting down my thoughts. I'm not sure how this writing will conclude.

Throughout this piece, I've used phrases like 'Let me tell you,' 'As I told you,' 'I already told you above,' and 'Let me clarify.' So, if you happen to read this, I'm uncertain how you'll interpret it, or what I should advise you about it. Just allow me to express myself, to share what's on my mind and in my heart. It might sound a bit unusual, but believe me, the joy of being true to yourself is indescribable. So, be authentic in everything you do.

They say you have to have an aim, target, or ambition for whatever you do. They say all your acts should have some purpose; the efforts you take should be made in a direction where you intend to achieve something. But at times, what I feel is that one must really go aimless; just enjoy doing what you do without actually caring about the outcome or aiming for the target. Like a kid does, and see how light and joyful you will be. So, what I am doing right now, while writing this, is giving me great pleasure. I am experiencing my childhood once again. Once again, I am going to school. Once again, I am playing with my schoolmates, who, in reality, are only there in my memory. Once again, I am travelling back to those places that have gone into oblivion for me now.

And, of course, the reason behind all this is that Centre Boy, whom I had seen at the bus stop while I was waiting for my company bus on August 15th, 2010, made me meet myself. Here, I thank him, from the bottom of my heart, for making it possible for me to meet myself, which otherwise would have been very difficult.

I think it's getting too much philosophical, so let's move on from here.

Now, let's revisit my childhood crush. But before I delve into that, you might be wondering, "Everything was going well so far, where did this childhood crush come from?" Well, let me clarify. This is the first time I'm sharing this. So, it's a pleasant afternoon, and it's September 16, 2010, when I resumed my writing and reflections. I had taken a brief break due to some recent commotion. Currently, I find myself at Delhi Airport, waiting for my next flight.

In front of me, there's a young girl, perhaps around eight or nine years old. She has an olive skin tone with a slightly wheatish complexion and sports two long braids. She's completely engrossed in her own world, playing in a way that occasionally prompts her parents to yell and shout, although it's all out of concern. They say things like, "Don't go there," "Play here," and "Stay in this area." But the little girl seems unaffected, lost in her own world without a care for the rest of the world, including her parents.

I couldn't help but smile as I watched her, and I eventually walked away to the nearby snack corner, feeling a bit hungry. After satisfying my hunger, I returned to my seat, waiting for my next flight. A little while later, the little girl and her parents disappeared, yet I still wore that gentle, contented smile. This was the moment that transported me back to a particular phase of my life, the one I'm sharing in this part of my writing.

Now, returning to the topic of 'childhood crush,' I want to clarify that I have no intention of writing a love story. In my view, a childhood crush is someone you never forget throughout your life. It's that moment when you first gaze at someone and then bashfully look away, capturing the innocence and beauty of that feeling. Importantly, it has nothing to do with matters of sex, bonding, emotions, or being together. This is a time when you have no inkling about what sex even is, nor do you comprehend the complexities of love and life.

Childhood crush—a girl whom I hesitate to mention because I am not in touch with her or any of my schoolmates from that time. I admit, I am somewhat apprehensive to write about her. I won't reveal any names, as I haven't done so thus far. However, if I describe the character, some of those who read this might make a guess.

Nevertheless, I'll continue. A gentle smile graces my face as I pen this down. I was in the fifth grade when I started to feel a certain way about a girl. Understand, at that age, such feelings had no depth, no emotional scale, no measurements of love. It was merely a sense that I enjoyed seeing her and having her around, much like how a child gets happy when playing with a favorite toy or encountering a familiar face that makes them feel secure and content. I realize this may seem repetitive, but I'm justifying it for those who might not grasp the simplicity of a child's affection.

I want to make one thing perfectly clear: there was no question of love or anything of the sort in this situation. After all, what does a child understand? There was no love, physical attraction, or such notions involved. Now, let's return to the little girl I saw at the airport. Yes, you've got it right; she reminded me of another girl who was in the same class as me. I can't pinpoint the first time I saw her, but she had the same angelic quality as the little girl at the airport – an olive-skinned complexion with slightly wheatish features and two long braids. But there was more to her. She excelled in her studies as well.

So, why did I have these feelings for her? Let me explain. Above all, I felt a bit envious of her. You see, she happened to be the daughter of someone in the school's management. Being from an influential family came with certain advantages, whether real or perceived. Occasionally, this privilege would manifest in her behavior. I must quickly apologise because I might be mistaken in my observations. I'm not trying to defame anyone. What I'm doing is simply recounting the thoughts of a child who couldn't help but notice the social dynamics at play, particularly when a classmate came from a well-off family. As I mentioned, I felt a twinge of envy due to her family background.

Now, I had plenty of reasons to be envious of her, but to be honest, I admired her and would often do so from a distance. I admired her simple and modest appearance, the way she carried herself, and her way of speaking. However, I find myself a bit puzzled as I write this. I'm not sure whether I should praise her or... well, I'm not sure what to write here.

But here's my only confession: that feeling of envy—yes, I'm using 'envy' instead of 'jealousy' because, as a child, I simply wished I could have the status she had. I would imagine that had my father been in a similar position in the school's management, or back then, when we were kids and didn't quite understand the concept of a management body, if he had owned the school, I would have behaved like this, or like that, been polite and humble, and so on. So, coming back to my confession, after all I've said about her, I truly admired that girl for three 'S's': her simplicity, soberness, and skillfulness.

Let me offer another apology. I may have sounded a bit sarcastic in what I wrote earlier about the girl. And this is what, my friends, I want to tell you today: after nearly seventeen or eighteen years that I'm still so uncertain about what I should actually be conveying about her. You can imagine my state of mind back then.

What I want to emphasize is that I can still vividly remember her face and may hardly ever forget it for the rest of my life. I don't know where she is now, but I can only wish, Wherever she is now, may she be happy.

As I write this, I'm filled with excitement and a deep immersion in so many memories from that time - memories of her, that class, the school, and my schoolmates. These memories are all clamoring to find their way onto the paper, and I'm worried that I might forget or miss some of them while trying to capture them in words. I almost wish I could narrate them and have someone write them down as fast as possible.

Right now, I'm completely lost in that pool of memories from that time, with that girl at the center of it all. And yes, I won't lie, it's bringing me peace and making me feel good as I reminisce about that phase of my life.

Then, the announcement for "Indigo passengers" broke me out of that sweet reverie, and with a gentle smile on my face and the image of that girl in my mind, I made my way to the Airbus.

But don't worry, by now, I've locked all those memories in my mind, never to forget them for the rest of my life. I'll take you through those moments in the writing that lies ahead.

"Kahin karti hogi vo mera intezaar, jiski tamanna mein firta hu bekaraar..." I couldn't resist the urge to listen to an old song as I already told you that I deeply love the old songs. It took me no time to take out my headphones and start playing this song that perfectly matched my reflections. With a smile on my face, I sank into the seat of the airbus.

"Sir, would you like to have something?" The air hostess interrupted my musical reverie to offer something to eat. With a smile, I whispered to myself, "Now, what should I ask you, ma'am?" and then returned to my song. "Sorry? What did you say, sir?" She responded politely but in a slightly high pitch. "No, nothing. Thank you!" I replied and went back to enjoy my song; what a lovely song, just go and listen to it now.

So this marks the end, or should I say, the start of that phase of my life, which this part of the write-up is about. But don't worry, I won't only write about that. I attended that school from the fourth grade until the seventh, so there are plenty of incidents and memories that keep flashing in front of my eyes. I'll do my best to take you through them, but many of them are connected to her.

And let me share one more thing—she was the reason behind my exit from this school after the seventh grade. No, don't jump to conclusions; please have patience and read on.

But for now, I'm smiling as I bring my emphasis on childhood crush to a close. I understand you might have been a bit bored, but for me, I'm smiling and content, although I'm not entirely sure why, especially since I haven't had any contact with her. But one thing is certain: I can't forget her.

Those Precious School Days

It's the 22nd of September 2010, 11:55 p.m. I've just arrived at the company to begin my night shift, starting around 11:30 p.m. I took over from the previous shift engineer, allocated work to the staff, and now I'm back in the office room. My work responsibilities are sorted, and I find myself diving into the past.

Now, you might be wondering, "If this guy is just sitting in the office room, revisiting his past, when does he actually work? Is he even doing his job?" I'm aware these questions might cross your mind, but my response to all of them can be summed up in one thing: a gentle smile.

I'm smiling at all your questions, but don't worry. Before you start labeling me as a slacker or *'kaamchor,'* give me a little time, and I'll provide the answers you need. I don't intend to justify my actions; rather, I want you to understand my journey and the reasons behind it. As I mentioned earlier, when I met myself on August 15th, 2010, I made a decision to embrace every moment, stage, and phase I've experienced. That means I want to travel through my life's journey from the furthest past to today. So hang in there, and let's continue.

Returning to the topic of this part of my write-up—my life and those precious school days—I'm taking a trip back to my fourth grade. By this point, I had become more at ease because I knew that the 'dhoti-kurta' was the uniform of a specific class teacher. All other teachers and students wore the standard attire of shirts and pants. So, my earlier confusion and fear had disappeared, and I was a happier kid on my way to school.

Let me paint a picture of the school campus and its surroundings, focusing on the smaller campus catering to the first through fourth standards. It consisted of a small single-story building with approximately five to six classrooms, or perhaps just four, one section for each standard. My fourth-grade classroom, as I entered at that level, faced a small road that separated the smaller campus from the larger one, which accommodated the fifth through tenth standards.

In front of my classroom, there stood a *'Chichbillai'* tree, bearing fruits known as 'Manila Tamarind.' Interestingly, I had never known the English name for this fruit until I wrote this. We used to relish these fruits. Adjacent to our school was a school for mentally disabled children.

There was a sugar candy vendor who I can still vividly recall standing right in front of our school. I should mention that he was a constant presence throughout the four years I spent there.

And last but certainly not least, especially for me, was the proximity of the childhood crush's house. Yes, things would indeed revolve around her, as I mentioned earlier, and now I am smiling again.

So, let me share with you my fourth-grade experience. As a newly admitted student, I had very few friends, familiar faces who mostly included a couple of my cousin sisters. I can't recall precisely if both were there from the fourth grade, or if one joined in the fifth. However, one thing is certain: when I left that school after completing the seventh grade, I had three of my cousin sisters studying in the same class as I. As far as my memory goes, two of them were there from the fourth class, while the third joined from the fifth in the adjacent campus.

Recalling my fourth-grade memories, I found myself under the guidance of that gentleman, yes, the one with the dhoti-kurta attire, as our class teacher.

I had a reputation as a good student, or at least that's what my parents believed, and they still do, and I can't help but smile. I carried the weight of high academic expectations, even though, compared to my siblings and cousins, I was just reasonably good at studying. For the past three years, I had consistently secured good marks and ranked among the top three students in my class. So, when I arrived in Nagpur, I carried the same image, and everyone, especially my family, had the same high expectations for me to maintain.

However, one fateful day, everything came crashing down, and I was left shattered. For a child like me at the time, it felt like the world had ended. The incident had such a profound impact on my young heart and mind that tears welled up and streamed down my face the entire day.

What was this incident, you ask? Well, hold on, because today I look back with deep regret and wish that it had happened again and again, even a thousand times over. Our class teacher, the very same dhoti-kurta gentleman, had a unique way of punishing his students. If a student made a mistake or failed to do their homework, the punishment was to have a boy sit in the girls' row, and vice versa. In our classroom, we all sat on cotton mats on the floor. Trust me, back in 1991–1992, this punishment felt like a death sentence to us. And on that day, I was sentenced to this 'gallows.' I was made to sit between two girls. I can't remember the exact reason for my punishment, but the embarrassment would have been less or I might have enjoyed it a bit if one of those girls was childhood crush. But to worsen the situation, one of the girls I sat between was my cousin.

On that day, it felt like all my dreams were crushed, and as I mentioned before, the world came crashing down. It might seem like a small matter now, something to smile or even laugh about, but for a child, it was a big event. Throughout that fateful day, I couldn't hold back my tears; they flowed continuously from the moment I was made to sit between two girls. Meanwhile, my fellow students took the opportunity to entertain themselves, laughing, smiling, and teasing me.

In that situation, I had a few concerns running through my childish mind. First, it was a sudden and unexpected blow to the image I had as a studious kid. Second, it was a humiliating experience to be seated between two girls, although today, I might have enjoyed it, as I previously mentioned, and now I regret that it didn't happen more often. Third, I was worried that my two cousins who were in the same class might spread the news within the family. Fourth, just to clarify, none of the girls involved were childhood crush – I'm just kidding.

With all these thoughts and emotions swirling around, I felt lost and spent the day cursing the heavens for letting that day happen.

I want to share one more thing, even though I'm a bit skeptical if I should mention it here. As a kid facing that unforgettable day, I found myself whispering curses about that dhoti-kurta teacher, saying to myself, *"Sala Budha, lavakar mela pahije."* (A mean old man... may he die soon). Needless to say, I was just a child.

I'd like to offer a heartfelt apology for those thoughts, which, in retrospect, were quite unkind. So, if you're out there, sir, I'm genuinely sorry for my childish behavior. It's 2010, almost twenty years later, I'm not certain where that teacher is, what he's doing, or even if he's still alive; wait, oh no... may God bless him with a long and healthy life. Back in 1991, when he taught us, he was already in his sixties so today he could be in his eighties.

Back to the incident: On that day, when I returned home, I was very down and out. I came home and straight away went to bed without talking to anyone in the family of seventeen-eighteen; of course, a few of the members were out on their assignments.

So, without saying a single word to anyone, I went to bed, of course, crying. "Sister-in-law, Bala is crying," yelled one of my aunts.

"See, what happened?"

"Kay zal, beta?" (What happened, child?), my mom asked.

"Kahi nahi, aai" (nothing, Mom.) I replied.

"Arey m ka radtos?" (Then, why are you crying?) She inquired back.

"Ag sangitl na kahi nahi zalay mhanun... Tu jaa barr mala zop yetey." (I told you, Mom, nothing has happened; you please go. I am feeling sleepy), I shouted at her.

And she, like every mother, said, *"Okay, beta, tu aram kar... kahi lagl tar mi ahe ithe."* (Ok, child, you relax yourself; if anything is needed, I am here).

Isn't it remarkable how a mother's character shines through? Even when I yelled at her, she remained calm and smiling, always ready to support me. To all of you reading this, take a moment to appreciate your mother, even for no particular reason, because as you read this, you've grown up. Do you really need a reason to show your gratitude to your mom? Take a moment to reflect.

After a few hours of rest, I woke up, perhaps around 3-4 p.m., and one of my worries had come true. The news had already spread within the family and among friends. Nowadays, we often discuss how communication technology has advanced, causing a revolution in our means of communication. But back in 1991, it felt incredibly swift. Well, maybe I'm just joking.

My mother asked me, *"Acha tula mulinchya ranget basval mhanun radat hota?"* (Were you crying because they made you sit with the girls?).

I wondered how she knew. It didn't take long for me to figure out her source of information. I began to view my cousin sisters in the same light as that teacher, secretly thinking, *'Agau ahet… kay garaz hoti sangayachi?'* (Were they being overly clever in sharing this at home?)

My mother inquired again, *"Arey mulinchya ranget basval mhanun radat hota."* (Were you crying because they made you sit with the girls?)

I replied, *"Ho, Aai."* (Yes, mother).

She comforted me, saying, *"Thik ahe na beta, kay zal tar, zau de."* (Alright, no worries, forget it.)

Suddenly, I felt at home and at ease. What I hadn't mentioned earlier was my biggest concern – the possible wrath of my mother upon my return to home from school.

But that wasn't there, and she was quite 'babying' me. *"Tyat kay zal tar, tu kiti vela ghari nahi ka tainsobat basto,"* (What's the big deal with that? Don't you sit with your cousin sisters at home?) she consoled. And I was happy, only to show her after hearing those words from her. However, at the back of my mind, this incident wasn't the one that was going down well with me.

Anyway, I can't forget this episode for the rest of my life, nor the teacher who had punished me in that manner, certainly not out of hatred. I'm smiling as I recall it.

Although I don't remember many incidents from the fourth grade, there are a few that have left a lasting impression on me. One such incident that comes to mind happened on a fine Friday. Every Friday, we had a Goddess Saraswati Puja, followed by the prayer *'Ya-kundedu,'* and then the program would conclude with *'Paasayadan.'* Of course, we would have *prasad* at the end, which was usually *'Gul-futane,'* a sweet treat made from gram and jaggery. I'd like to emphasize that our *prasad* was healthy, unlike today, where fast food and unhealthy beverages are often offered as *prasad*. I'm not promoting or criticising any particular product or food choice; I'm merely stating the difference.

So, on that Friday, after finishing the puja, we boys went out to play. While playing, I'm not sure what came over me, but I playfully threw a stone, actually a *'Gitti,'* which was a small angular rock or ballast, at one of my friends. Unfortunately, it hit him square in the middle of his nose. He sat down in shock, both hands covering his nose because I had thrown it from a fair distance, and he didn't know who had thrown the stone.

I ran over to him, concerned about whether he was hurt badly. When I reached him, he was still on the ground, hands covering his entire face, especially his nose. Just as I was about to ask if he was okay, he suddenly stood up, hands off his nose, and all I saw was blood. His nose and the surrounding area were covered in blood, and it was still bleeding.

He was terrified and crying, but my fear was different. I was more scared, but I wasn't crying. At that moment, my fear was something else entirely. A couple of students hurried inside to inform the school authorities about the incident.

Suddenly, a few teachers came out and took the injured boy inside, leaving me in a state of shock. At that moment, my concerns were quite different. Various thoughts raced through my mind: Did anyone witness me throwing the stone? Is his injury serious? Will his family come to school to find out who did this? And many more questions. However, what scared me the most were these questions: What if the police gets involved? Will they arrest me? Will I end up behind bars?

I went home that day with a confused, scared, and panic-stricken mind, feeling extremely nervous. The next day, the injured boy returned to school with a bandage on his nose, and he was perfectly fine. I breathed a sigh of relief. To this day, no one else knows who threw the stone except me.

Regardless, I'm no longer in contact with that boy, but, *dost* (pal), wherever you are, I want to say that I'm deeply sorry for that incident. I never intended to hurt you; it was just a playful act gone wrong. Sorry.

Now, onto the third and final incident I remember, although I'm not entirely sure if it happened when I was in fourth or fifth grade. As far as my memory takes me, it was during my fourth-grade year.

I tried to recall whether the incident I'm about to share happened in my fourth or fifth grade, closing my eyes to visualize the moment. A single image was formed in my memory, suggesting it occurred during my fourth-grade year. There was still a hint of doubt, but the exact grade wasn't important. What matters is the incident itself.

This story revolves around childhood crush, as I've hinted earlier, and, as promised, I'm connecting these tales around her. However, this time, it's not just about her but her mother is also involved.

So, childhood crush had been absent from school for a few days, and I couldn't help but worry. Even though my deeper feelings for her developed in the fifth grade, I had started to notice her in the middle of my fourth standard. I just wanted her to be present and around, which made her absence a cause for concern.

One day, while she was still away, I spotted her mother engaged in a conversation with our class teacher right in front of our classroom. By this time, after nearly six or seven months in that school, I had come to recognize her parents' faces, though not all the family members. They resided very close to the school, as I mentioned earlier.

Seeing her mother talking to the teacher, I felt an urge to go and inquire about why my crush hadn't been coming to school.

Regardless, the question about crush's absence stayed, and I couldn't dare to inquire. It was only a few days later that I learned she had fallen sick with chickenpox, a condition we referred to as *'Devi-cha-rog'* back then.

I found myself praying to God for her speedy recovery and a return to school. Miraculously, it seemed the almighty heard me, and she did return to school. However, irony struck as soon as she started coming to her classes; I fell ill with the same *'Devi-cha-rog,'* or chickenpox. It was my turn to rest at home, and I couldn't help but exclaim, *"Bhagwan aap mahan ho."* (God, you are great). Smiling, I recall the sequence of events.

After the usual course of time required for chickenpox to subside, I also recovered and returned to school. Eventually, both of us, along with our fellow students, continued our fourth-grade journey until the summer vacation began. This marked the conclusion of my fourth-grade adventure in that school.

I'd like to share one thing that happened earlier today. During a chat with my mother this afternoon, I found myself asking her numerous questions about my childhood, my siblings, this school, and my friends who used to visit our home. To this, she jokingly responded, *"Ka re, baba, itk kay vichartoy… pustak vagere lihitoy kay?"* (What happened? Why are you asking so much? Are you writing a book?)

With a smile, I replied, *"Nahi g sahaj vicharl."* (No, no, I am just casually asking.)

Today, I discovered something I wasn't aware of before. It turns out that my sister attended a different school during this period. She joined the school where my brother and I were studying after spending a couple of years in another institution. Originally, I thought she was in the same school but in a different campus, as

I mentioned earlier. She joined this school when I was in the sixth grade, and she was in the eighth grade.

And so, as I look back and recall, I bring my fourth-grade journey to a close with a smile.

My memories from the fourth standard are a cherished collection:

The first day of school, a special day spent with my father.

The unforgettable Dhoti-Kurta Teacher.

The incident of sitting in the girls' lane.

A kid's irrational fear of the police due to a stone-pelting episode.

The entry of childhood crush into my life, that always brings a smile to my face.

Now, let's talk about the sweet summer vacation days. Today's children have a multitude of summer classes to choose from, including drawing, art, craft, singing, dancing, and more. But back in our time, summer vacations were meant for one thing—pure, unadulterated fun. We could be carefree kids, without the burden of classes and studies.

I can't help but feel sorry for today's kids who are often under pressure during their summer breaks. After ten months at school, they still have these so-called 'summer classes' to attend. While these classes have their benefits, I believe we should also allow kids to be kids during this precious time, letting them play, have fun, and enjoy their childhood.

During our summer vacation after completing the fourth grade, we children, eight from our house and more from neighboring homes played with boundless energy. Of course, this had its advantages and disadvantages. However, there's one particular memory that stays in my mind, and I can't help but smile when I think about it.

On one sunny afternoon, while our summer vacations were in full swing, we decided to play hide and seek. It was around four or five in the afternoon, and the children from the neighborhood gathered in the *'gullies,'* or the narrow lanes that separated our houses.

So one day, while I was running to seek while playing that game, I fell down badly and had a nasty blow to my mouth. A couple of my teeth were badly broken; they were in fact uprooted, and they were heavily bleeding. I can still recall that day and that moment. Because, as I got up, only I knew what it took to get back up; all I could see was a flow of blood coming out of my mouth, and I was yelling and crying. Someone called my rescuer, my mother, and I was immediately rushed to the hospital by my mother.

After undergoing the treatment, I still remember that for the next week or so, I could not play outdoor games and was asked to stay inside the home.

Now, why did I say earlier that this is the incident that I can never forget, and it will be there with me till I breathe my last...

As I told you, my teeth were badly hurt, and even after undergoing the treatment, today they remain misaligned and crooked.

And that's how the summer vacation ended, giving me an unforgettable memory, a lifetime memory, and misaligned teeth.

Back To The School

With the end of the summer vacation, school resumed its regular schedule. In those days, school shopping was a once-a-year event, unlike today when parents seem to be shopping for their kids almost every other day. For us, it was a time of great celebration as we prepared to go back to school. Mothers would take us shopping, and acquiring a school bag, a water bottle, and a compass box, along with books and notebooks, was more exciting to us than anything else.

We returned to school, now entering the fifth grade. This time, we moved to the larger campus located on the other side of the road. It was also the year we were introduced to a new subject, something we had never encountered before – 'English.' Unlike today, where kids learn English before they even learn to walk, in our days, we started learning English from the fifth grade.

Our English teacher was a strict lady. I remember her well. By this point, I had spent a year at the school, and I was familiar with most of the students. I had even made a few close friends. I'm going to try to remember all of them one by one.

The first friend who came to mind was a girl with albinism, a condition she likely had since birth. Her unique appearance made her easily recognisable. But, trust me, the way she behaved, for all those three years, as I wasn't knowing much of her in the fourth standard, I can say she was a bit egoistic, arrogant sort of girl.

I still remember an incident relating to her that made me feel like she was an egoist.

To tell you about that, it was our PT/PE class, and our teacher would often make us play one game during this class, of course, an outdoor game called *'Langadi.'* Now, I am not sure what this game is known as in English—in fact, I'm not even sure if it's played outside. But yes, it's played in various parts of India with various names.

To an extent, it may be more or less similar to hopscotch, though not exactly the same.

So, to tell you, in short, about the game and the way we used to play it, all the students, both the girls and the boys, would stand in such a way that they formed a circle. The match used to be between the boy's team and the girl's team. Three girls would be asked to roam freely in the circle, while a boy had to get catch hold of them, of course just by touching them, in the *'Langadi'* position (one leg to be lifted from the ground and in the air while you get catch hold of all the free-roaming girls reaching at them with the help of a grounded leg, jumping), and vice versa.

On that day, out of the three girls who were asked first to roam in the circle, one was this girl and I was the boy, and I was asked to oust them. As I was making my efforts, of course in the *'Langadi'* position, to touch them and get them out, I unintentionally hit this girl on her forearm. And it hardly took any time for the affected area of her forearm to turn 'red' as she was already too fair.

After the game concluded, she approached one of my friends who happened to be her neighbor, and yelled at him, "Hey, ask your friend to be more considerate when touching girls. He hit so hard; look at the red area!" She continued with, *"Pagal."* (mad).

The next friend who comes to mind is a guy who was physically challenged. To the best of my recollection, he was a new student. I don't remember seeing him during the fourth grade. It's possible that I hadn't crossed paths with him that year, or perhaps, I was new to the class, and I hadn't taken notice of him. Based on my memory, I can only say that he joined later during the fifth grade.

Being physically challenged, he couldn't walk and used a wheelchair. I don't recall much about him, but I distinctly remember one thing - I used to help him daily by carrying his school bag from the classroom to the office area. This was where his wheelchair would be parked or, perhaps, where someone from his family or an auto-rickshaw would pick him up after school. On his face, especially on the first day, I could see the anxiety of wondering who would carry his bag from the classroom when school ended. I decided to do it.

It would give me a lot of pleasure, not because I was helping him but because, at times, in turn, he would allow me to drive his wheeled chair. And that was a great joy for me. Understand one thing: all were kids, including me.

So it wasn't anything like playing with someone's emotions or something. Today, while reading, you might feel so. Even a few might object that this is nothing but making fun of that guy, but trust me, all of us, including that guy himself, would really enjoy doing all this.

The third one, of course, was a guy who was residing adjacent to this girl—yes, that fair-skinned girl. I recall this fellow prominently because we used to go a lot to his home after school hours, as his home was on the way back to our home from school. For all those three years, almost every day, we would go to him after school hours and play for an hour or two, and then we would go back home.

The next fellow that I recall is a guy whose father used to deal in comic books. Yes, in those times, we were crazy about having those comic books on rent, maybe for a day or two, read them, enjoy them, and return them.

We had a couple of guys near our home who would lend us these comic books on rent. But, as it wasn't that affordable to us, we found a solution, and it was this guy.

I made him one of my close friends, not only to have those books free of charge but because he was a good guy too. We would go to this guy as well and play at him. But because he would stay a bit away, it wasn't a regular affair to visit him; rather, he would be at us almost daily on the way back home from school.

One memory that I vividly recall of this fellow is that he would bring '*Murmure*' or 'puffed rice' with some spices in it, which would taste really awesome. I think my love for this item developed then and there.

Thereafter, a girl happened to be the benchmate of the childhood crush. Yes, she was also one of the studious girls we had in that class. Of course, I was also one of them. This girl was a close friend of childhood crush. Since she lived near childhood crush's home, in the school, they got along quite well. You could see the two of them hand in hand almost all the time.

For us, she was the companion of the 'heavyweight' – childhood crush. Consequently, she was like the school's default owner. Needless to say, besides being a good student, she was also good-looking.

There was a girl in our class who happened to be the daughter of one of our teachers. However, I don't have many vivid memories of her because she was quite silent and introverted.

There was also a boy who was one of my close friends, and the reason was quite unique – he had a dark complexion like mine. So, whenever other students teased me about my skin colour, I had a strong ally in him. Yes, there were times when I would complain to the Almighty about why I wasn't fair-skinned like the other students in the school. However, that complaint remained unanswered until I reached an age where I started understanding the importance of a complete person, realising that my grievances were unwarranted. Needless to mention, we already had that physically challenged fellow in our class.

Another fellow I remember was the one, at whom we used to attend the tuition classes, held by our lady class teacher.

Three more girls come to mind now... They were, of course, my cousin sisters. So, if I set aside these three sisters, I am not in contact with any of the characters I recalled. I just don't know where they are, what they are doing, or if they remember me. Perhaps, they wouldn't even recognize me if we crossed paths again. With all these question marks in my mind, I am...

My mother gently inquired, *"Arey zopla nahi ka?"* which translates to, "Hey, haven't you gone to bed yet?" It's 24th September 2010, 10:30 pm. I'm a bit unwell, so I haven't gone to the night shift at the office. To be honest, it's not sickness that's keeping me up but nervousness. I won't delve into the reasons now, but I'm going to bed with a smile. Goodnight.

Good afternoon, it's 25th September 2010, and I'm at home, just relaxing.

Returning to my fifth-grade memories, as I mentioned, we had a very strict lady as our class teacher this time, and we lived in fear of what would happen on days when we hadn't completed our homework.

One fine day, I faced the rage of that teacher. It was just the beginning of the fifth standard, about fifteen to twenty days in, and we were asked to memorize the English alphabet. I went to school that day with my homework done, but little did I know that I would be the one in her firing line.

As she began to go around the classroom, asking each of us to recite the alphabet, my heart raced. And then, it was my turn. "Mam... 'A... B... C... G...'" But the next sound that filled the room was a resounding "Dhummm." Yes, you're right, that was the sound that echoed as she bent me over, holding my hair, and delivered a firm smack to my back. She exclaimed, *"Murkha... abhyas nahi kela!"* (Silly boy, you didn't do the homework). Now, you can imagine that for a boy who had already faced embarrassment by sitting in the girls' lane, this felt like going to the gallows.

I felt like it was the end of my school life, and I was in tears. When I made eye contact with my sisters and a few close friends, they were smiling at me, though they were undoubtedly filled with fear as well since it was soon their turn.

And that's why I mentioned above how I could never forget that lady, yes, my teacher. However, one thing I'd like to emphasize is that by the time I left that school, I was one of the few students who were in her good books. Today, I'm not sure where she is, if she still teaches in that school, or if she's still as strict as she was back then.

This incident was the turning point that sparked my love for English. It was after this event that I decided to be more focused and attentive toward this subject, which had been missing from my life until the fourth grade.

My mother deserves credit as my savior that day. When I returned home, I was feeling quite upset and nervous, as was my usual state. My mother noticed and asked me about what had happened at school that day. Without any delay, I narrated the entire incident to her, saying, *"Aai, A—B—C—D path nahvati keli na, mhanun marl madam ne."* (Mom, I was scolded by the teacher because I didn't learn and recite the A-B-C-D). She calmly responded, *"Mag karayachi ki,"* (Then you should do it) calming me down. I assured her by saying, *"Ho Aai, nakki karil,"* (Yes, mother, I will definitely do it) and we hugged. It's needless to say that the very next day, I went to school with that homework properly completed.

"Bala, chaha ghe," (Bala, have a cup of tea), "and see what the civil contractor is saying," yelled my mom. There's some construction work happening at our home, including the construction of two more floors. I'm now going to have my afternoon tea, but I'll be back later. So, goodbye for now.

By the way, my nickname is 'Bala'. I'm not sure if I've mentioned that before.

A Scary Incident And A Lesson For Life

I can't recall the exact day, but as a child, I was profoundly affected by an incident. It was after school hours, and I was playing with a few friends in the vicinity of our school. Our school was situated near a heavily crowded avenue, about 100-150 feet away from the school's boundary.

On that particular day, instead of heading home, I and some of my friends decided to play nearby. I remember being momentarily separated from the other boys, finding myself in a nearby lane. I ended up behind a group of *Hijras* or *Kinnars* who were passing by. I can't recall the exact game we were playing, but I was waiting for the group to pass so I could rejoin my friends.

Suddenly, a truck came up from behind and attempted to overtake the group. The lane was quite narrow, with one side slightly raised due to some materials on the side, causing the truck to tilt. Before I could fully comprehend what was happening, the truck toppled over, landing on one of the members of the *Hijra* group. The scene I witnessed shook me to my core, leaving me completely devastated.

The aftermath was chaotic. The group erupted into shouts, cries, yells, and curses, and for a child like me, it was a terrifying experience. It was challenging to grasp the full extent of what had occurred. Soon, a crowd of people gathered around the accident site, and driven by both curiosity and fear, I, too, approached to see what had transpired.

I found myself surrounded by a pool of blood and hastily fled the scene. Now, why am I recounting this incident or why is it on my mind? There isn't anything particularly significant about the incident itself, but I feel compelled to share it here. So, let me clarify why I'm mentioning this incident.

As I mentioned earlier, this incident had a profound impact on me. When I returned home, I was filled with questions, fear, doubt, and various emotions. I won't go into all the details here, as I don't want to delve into a serious mood unnecessarily.

What I want to convey is that I was in deep fear after that incident, to the extent that I couldn't even eat for two to three days. I was reluctant to attend school. It felt like my life had come to a standstill. The pain, sorrow, grief, and the sounds of that day haunted me.

But once again, my savior—my mother, came to my rescue. She took charge of the situation and asked me to narrate what had happened because I had stopped talking to anyone in the house. Finally, I shared the incident with her, and she reassured me, saying, *"Bala, bagh te radat hote, ordat hote karan tyanchya mitrala lagl hot na."* (Bala, those people were upset because their friend was badly hurt. They were expressing their grief.)

"When something doesn't go our way in life, we're unhappy, and if we're unhappy, we cry." She continued to explain various aspects of life, including its joys, happiness, sorrows, grief, and ups and downs, and I became engrossed in her words.

As a child, I found it a bit challenging to fully grasp the message my mother was conveying, especially in relation to the episode I had witnessed. However, the primary lesson I took away from that day was a simple yet profound one: this is what life is all about.

Whenever I reflect on that incident, I can't help but smile, realising that there is no person on this planet who has only experienced laughter or tears throughout their entire life. Life is a mix of joy, sorrow, happiness, and moments of anxiety. It encompasses the scorching heat of the sun as well as the soothing embrace of the rain.

Time, I've come to understand, is like an elixir. It possesses the power to heal almost everything. It serves as a solution to most problems, and if it isn't, it at least fades the scars of those problems with the passage of time, offering a new ray of hope.

On that day, my mother imparted a vital life lesson to me: to never give up and to not be crushed by the pressures of the situation or condition. She taught me that even when life's incidents may shake you or leave you feeling broken, the key is to stand tall, stand firm, and, with time, emerge victorious.

In any case, I expressed my gratitude to my mother, saying, *"Aai tu kiti changlli ah g... mala kiti prem karte, maza lad karte, mala barr nasl ki kadewar dawakhanyat nete, Aai tu kiti karte g mazya sathi... tula trass nahi ka hot....."* (Mom, you are incredibly kind. You love me deeply, and you take me to the hospital when I'm unwell. I appreciate everything you do for me. Do you ever get tired? Do you ever feel the strain of all this?) I said this while hugging her tightly.

She responded by saying, *"Bala, sonya ahe re tu maza."* (Bala, you are my baby, dear). She held me tightly as she spoke those words.

These are just a few of the memories I have from my fifth grade. While there are many more, some are challenging to recall or include here. But yes, it was a sweet start to my next two classes, which I completed at that school after the fifth grade.

Looking back on my fifth-grade experiences, several distinct memories stand out. First and foremost, having a particularly stern class teacher during that year. The memory of her strict demeanour remains vivid in my mind. Another noteworthy recollection revolves around the incident where I had to diligently memorize and learn the A-B-C-D, a challenge that left a lasting impression. Then the unforgettable accident that occurred during that time, which significantly impacted me. However, one of the long-lasting memories from that year is the invaluable life lesson I received from my savior, my mother, who imparted wisdom about the essence of life. These recollections collectively shape my reminiscences of my fifth-grade year.

An Unforgettable Sweet Rainy Morning

Hello! It's October 2, 2010, and I found myself having dinner, or perhaps I should call it a meal, during the second shift at the company canteen, around 7:15 p.m. Unexpectedly, I received a call from our general manager, who also happened to be our plant head.

He said, "Akhil, listen, you have to go to Ludhiana tomorrow."

I replied, "Sir, I am actually off tomorrow," albeit not very firmly.

He emphasised, "It's urgent."

Unwillingly, I agreed, saying, "Okay, sir." After that, I promptly informed my Head of Department (HOD) about the situation. He responded, not in the best mood, "Ah, this boss again! Sending you for the tenth time."

I explained, "Sir, he is sending me again."

"Okay, hand over the shift responsibilities to the other engineer and head home because you will have to catch a morning flight to Delhi and then proceed to Ludhiana by train," said my HOD.

I replied, "Okay, sir," this time with a hint of relief. Though I was initially annoyed and irritated by the phone call, I saw it as an opportunity to prove myself after facing challenges and internal conflicts. As I mentioned earlier, I wanted to embrace every moment of my life, and this was just another one of those moments.

On October 3, 2010, a Sunday, I took a flight to Delhi and relaxed in my seat, contemplating my journey. Now, let's delve into the main topic of this section: "An unforgettable sweet rainy morning." I can't pinpoint the exact date, but I was in the sixth grade at that time.

On one fine day in July or August 1993 maybe, it was raining heavily in the morning. But, before that, let me tell you one thing, in those days, there were no school buses or transportation services like today. So students like me had to walk to school independently, without parental assistance.

My mother inquired, *"Bala, far paus yetoy, tu janar ki nahi shalet?"* (Bala, since it's raining, will you go to school today?). I replied, *"Aai, kami zalay thoda, mi janar"* (Mother, the rain has subsided a bit, so I'll go).

No, no, don't get me wrong; I wasn't exactly known for being a diligent or punctual student. On that particular day in fact, as it was raining, I thought there wouldn't be too many students attending school, but childhood crush as she would stay quite close to the school.

So I just took my mini-umbrella and embarked on the three to four-kilometer journey to school. Halfway there, it started to rain again, and this time, more heavily, rendering my small umbrella virtually useless. I ended up thoroughly drenched and had to navigate waterlogged streets.

Upon finally arriving at the school campus, still dripping wet but relieved, my anxiety transformed into a smile. My joy stemmed from spotting childhood crush's best friend standing outside the classroom, observing the rain. The school's campus was comparatively small by today's standards.

My delight wasn't solely because I had seen her; it was due to my expectation that many students might be absent due to the heavy rain. I hadn't observed a significant gathering of students upon entering the school gate, which made me happy to see her friend at the classroom door. In my mind, I presumed that if her friend was there, crush might be inside the classroom. This assumption brought me joy, as it seemed that both of them had braved the rain to come to school, likely because they lived nearby.

It's hard to put into words just how ecstatic I felt on that rainy morning. With only a few students present, heavy rain, and perhaps a shortage of teachers, there were no classes, which meant more time for fun and mischief. This also meant more opportunities to interact with 'her'.

Let me clarify something. She held a special place in the school due to her heavyweight status as the owner's daughter. Meanwhile, my jealousy and inferiority complex served as tools for my stubborn, arrogant, and self-obsessed behavior. I never initiated a conversation with her, and I can't even recall a single moment when we talked openly, except for academic matters that involved the entire class, including the teacher.

She never initiated a conversation with me either, which wasn't surprising. The feeling of inferiority held me back from approaching her. Instead, I occasionally conversed with her friend. On that particular day, as I entered, I smiled at her friend, who reacted as if to say, *"Arey, bhijla purn tu"* (You're completely drenched).

Returning to my emotions, as I neared the classroom and saw her friend waiting outside, I entered the realm of fantasy. However, it was short-lived because when I entered the classroom, all I saw was her friend's school bag, with no other students, let alone her.

I exclaimed, *"Shit yaar, kunich nahi and ti pan nahi"* (Oh no, no one's here, not even her). So, why do I call it a 'sweet rainy morning'? It was 'rainy' because of the rain, and 'sweet' because, despite the considerable effort and anticipation, I had reached the school, saw her friend outside, and momentarily immersed myself in a world of fantasy, anticipating her being inside.

You know, it's hard for me to make you understand the depth of emotions a child like me felt during those three to four minutes. I cherish that moment whenever I recall it—a memory that I'll never forget. You see, it's impossible to grasp the emotions of that child I once was.

Time To Say 'Bye-Bye' To The School

After spending three remarkable years in the school, covering the fourth, fifth, and sixth standards, I had developed a childhood crush, made some wonderful friends, and collected countless memories. However, it was time for me to bid farewell to this school, even though it offered classes up to the tenth standard, just as it did for my siblings and cousins.

You might wonder why I left the school after only completing the sixth standard. The reason for my departure was linked to childhood crush, but not directly because of her. Instead, it was influenced by her background and the treatment I received on a particular day at school due to not having any significant connections, which wounded my self-esteem, pride, and, you could say, ego to an extent.

On that day, I couldn't help but feel that if I had been the son of the school owner, I might have received special treatment, attention, and courtesy. Adding to my frustration was the special treatment that childhood crush's friend received, which only fueled my feelings.

To give you some context, I was among the top three students in the sixth standard, with the other two being childhood crush and her friend. Both of them were exceptionally bright and dedicated students, creating a competitive environment between us.

I use "between" instead of "among" because they formed one party in this rivalry. They were not just the class toppers but also the school toppers. However, I was no slouch when it came to my studies. In the preceding fourth and fifth standards, I had already made a name for myself as one of the studious students.

In the sixth standard, the competition between childhood crush, her friend, and me was fierce. I won't mention the specific order in which we ranked, mainly because I don't remember it now, and I smile as I admit this.

Today, to be frank, I don't attach much importance to the grading system and marks. But back in those days, it was our entire world, and for a few days, after achieving top rankings, we were on cloud nine.

So, after securing a spot in the top three, I eagerly anticipated the same treatment I observed my two classmates receiving. As our seventh standard began after the summer vacation, we all gathered on the first day of school. There was a recap of the previous year, and the applause and attention they received made me intensely jealous and fueled feelings of inferiority.

I had observed this for the past three years, but in the fourth standard, both were new to each other, The school and I, but in the fifth standard, I had already established myself as a studious student. In the sixth standard, I managed to rank among the top three. I believed that I would finally be recognized in the school just like them.

I must note that when I mention the treatment being received, I want to exclude one teacher, the strict lady teacher, because I had already earned her favour by that time. I'm not trying to defame the other teachers, students, or staff, but the fact remains the same, with only a few close friends exempted from this observation.

I began to feel inferior and started thinking, *"Kash, mi pan hichya sarkha shrimant asto, ani hi mazya papanchi shala asti"* (If only I were as wealthy as she was, and if my father were the owner of the school...). These thoughts troubled me, and I couldn't shake them off.

I want to clarify that I'm not trying to encourage discrimination, comparison, jealousy, or envy. Of course, whatever happened wasn't right, but let's remember, I was just a child.

Throughout that day, I remained withdrawn, unable to focus. After school, a few friends called out, *"Akhil, chal kheluya,"* (Akhil, let's play), but because I was already upset, I chose to go home instead of joining them.

That day, after getting back home, I was still down and nervous.

"*Kay zal bala?*" (What happened, Bala?) Mom inquired.

"*Aai mi nahi janar tya shalet, mala nahi avdat ti shala, sarv tilach hushar samjtat*" (Mom, I won't go to that school; I don't like that school; everyone thinks she is more studious). "*Arey kunabaddal boltoy?*" (Whom are you talking about?) asked my mother.

"*Ag tich, shalechya malkachi mulgi*" (the same girl, the daughter of the school owner), I replied.

"*Ani aai aaj tar farach zal*" (And, Mom, today it was too much).

"*Tichya maitrinila sudha khup talya milaya, pan mala nahi, mi pan tar pahilya tin madhe alo ahe na, Aai*" (Her mate also received a lot of clapping and applauding, but not me; I also stood in the top three, Mom.) I yelled.

"*Arey, Bala, kiti ragavtos, kiti chidtos*" (Hey, Bala, why do you get so angry?) said my mother, calming me down.

"*Nahi, tula sangitl na, mala nahi jayach tya shalet, mazz nav kadh tithun, ani dusrya shalet tak*" (I told you, I don't want to go to that school; please withdraw my name from that school and get me to some other school), said I, again shouting at her.

"*Barr barr, baba, pappana yeu de ratri, sangte, dusrya shalet tak mhanun tula, thik*" (Ok, let Papa come home tonight; I will ask him to send you to some other school, happy), said she, of course, again calming me down and pampering me.

And this was the day when my exit from the school was decided, of course, by me. So I hope that now you won't blame childhood crush for being the reason for my exit from that school.

That night, my mother called me, saying, *"Bala, beta ikde ye, Papa bolavit ahet tula"* (Bala, come here; Papa is calling), as my father was home and having his dinner. I went to both of them and sat with my father to have dinner.

One thing I want to emphasise is that I used to have dinner with my father from the same plate until I was sixteen or seventeen. I would have my dinner before he came home, but then I would wait for him to return and have something with him from the same plate. I just can't forget those days.

So that day, I sat with him while my mother sat beside us, serving us.

My father asked, *"Bala, kay zal beta, aai kay sangte?"* (Bala, what happened? What's your mother saying?)

I replied, *"Ho, Papa, mi nahi janar tya shalet,"* (Yes, Papa, I won't go to that school) in agreement with what he had heard from my mother.

My father replied, *"Arey pan tyat ragavnaysarkh kay ahe, tula pan shabaski milalich asel na, top alyabaddal?"* (Hey, what's there to get annoyed with? You might have received applause too for being the top student.)

I responded a bit firmly, *"Papa, aplyakade khup paise ka nahi? Aapan shrimant ka nahi?"* (Papa, why don't we have a lot of money? Why aren't we rich?)

I questioned, *"Tumchi shala ka nahi? Papa apli shala kadha, ani mala tithe taka"* (Why don't you own a school? Papa, build our own school and admit me there).

My father replied, *"Thik ahe, beta, tula dusrya shalet takto, pan aata ek varsh, mhanje satvi purn kar ki ithe, mag nakki tula takel dusrya shalet"* (Alright, beta, I'll send you to another school, but for now, complete your seventh standard here. After that, I'll definitely send you to another school), cuddling me.

"*Ho, papa,*" (Yes, papa) I exclaimed with immense joy. Trust me, in that moment, my happiness knew no bounds.

"*Chal ma ja zop ata,*" (Go and sleep now) my father told me.

"*Ho, papa,*" (Yes, Papa) I responded, running off to my siblings, still filled with excitement.

The next day, both of them seemed to have forgotten the previous night's episode, and it was just another ordinary morning for my parents.

But for me, I felt like I had the world at my feet after being assured of attending a new school. With a heart full of happiness, I eagerly headed to school as the usual seventh-grade academic session began.

An Incident Of That Year That's Coming To My Mind

We all, except for childhood crush and her friend, attended private tuition sessions from that strict lady teacher after our regular school hours. Perhaps it was because she was the daughter of the school owner and came from a well-off family. It's possible she attended a different, more expensive tuition class only due to financial reasons, as our teacher was known for her excellent teaching skills. Alternatively, she and her friend might have gone to a different teacher from our school. I'm not entirely sure.

Naturally, she didn't seem to favor our teacher for some reason. I can't pinpoint the exact cause, but I have a vivid memory of the day when childhood crush engaged in a heated argument with our teacher. The dialogue she had with the teacher that day both surprised and shocked me. I won't quote the exact words, but it became clear to me that it was due to her background.

I want to clarify that I'm not implying she had a particular upbringing, culture, or values from her family that made her act this way. However, when you have an advantage over others in some aspect, a feeling of superiority can unconsciously develop. It's not necessarily about her or her family possessing this superiority, but rather how people treat her, which in turn influences her perception of herself.

I want to stress that she was just a child, like me, and it wouldn't be fair to judge her or her family based on this incident. I smile as I think about it, understanding that such conflicts can happen to anyone, especially at a young age.

I want to clarify that I'm not taking her side, but the fact remains that we were all children at the time.

This incident led to me deciding to leave that school, essentially issuing myself an exit visa. Another incident pushed me towards this decision which eventually made my father going to the school to discuss obtaining my school leaving certificate. I became convinced that continuing my education in that school was not the right choice.

The incident I want to talk about occurred during the annual gathering, which usually took place in winter, possibly in January or February. During this event, students who performed well in the previous year were felicitated, typically by the Chief Guest, who happened to be the father of childhood crush.

Throughout my time at the school, it seemed like the only Chief Guests we had were members of her family, with a few exceptions that I can't recall. As I had performed well in the sixth standard, I had high hopes of receiving recognition and appreciation, if not a grand accolade, during the annual gathering.

However, my hopes and expectations were shattered when I saw childhood crush and her friend, who were also in the top three, stealing the spotlight. They were the center of attention, leaving me feeling like I was nowhere to be seen and receiving secondary treatment. I felt that it wasn't just my own dishonor but also a dishonor to my parents. I felt that they were being disrespected, ignored, and neglected.

I received a token of appreciation in the form of a compass box (I still remember its colour and appearance), but that was not all I desired. I wanted the teachers, staff, and Chief Guest to know me, and I wanted my parents to be recognized by my name.

Childhood crush's father, as the school owner, was well-known to everyone, and her friend, being her close companion and residing near the school, was equally familiar to all, along with their parents.

But where were my parents? They seemed lost among those heavyweights.

By that time, I was fragile and while I have been bendable, I would not have been easily swayed if anyone had tried to convince me to stay in the same school. Eventually, this situation prompted my father to go to school and get me out of that school after my seventh-grade year.

And thus I bid farewell to the lovely four years I spent at that lovely school. In the year 1995, I said goodbye to it, having passed the seventh grade.

The memories I carry from those four years of my life include the very first day at school, where I was skeptical about the Dhoti-Kurta uniform and the train track leading all the way to the school. I recall the Dhoti Kurta teacher, sitting in the girls lane, the sugar candy vendor, and the *'Chich-Billai'* or the 'Manila – Tamarind' tree. There was the episode of pelting a stone at a friend, which left me scared afterward. I also remember the A-B-C-D episode, the *'Langadi'* incident involving the fair-skinned girl, and the comics book dealer dad of one of my friends who offered puffed rice. There was the strict lady teacher and a physically challenged friend with his tricycle. And, of course, on top of it all, was childhood crush, who eventually, indirectly and unknowingly, became the reason for my departure from the school. As I share these memories today, I must admit that I'm no longer in contact with her, and I'm not sure if we'll ever meet again. If we do, which seems unlikely, I may find it challenging to share these recollections with her, but I smile at the thought.

A Trip To Mumbai

Having successfully completed my seventh standard and with my parents assuring me of enrolling in another school, I was on cloud nine during that summer vacation. My uncle, who still resides in Mumbai today, had come to Nagpur for some official work. Given that it was my summer break, he suggested I accompany him to Mumbai, and I eagerly agreed, saying, *"Ho kaka mi yenar tumchaysobat"* (Yes, Uncle, I will come with you to Mumbai).

Thus, I embarked on my first trip to Mumbai in the summer of 1995. While there wasn't much that stood out as exciting about this trip, I found myself experiencing a sense of loneliness during my stay. Both my uncle and aunt had to go to work, leaving my little cousin brother, who was my uncle's son, and me in the care of my aunt's mother, who lived a fifteen-minute walk away from my uncle's home.

This experience made me realize how people can become so engrossed in their work, including their office responsibilities, that they often find very little time for themselves, let alone for others. Today, I find myself residing and working in Nagpur, having spent about seven to eight months working in Pune in 2006–2007. However, I firmly decided to return to my native place and stay with my family, prioritising that connection over professional pursuits.

I want to clarify that I'm not suggesting you shouldn't leave your homes for work or jobs. What I want to convey is the importance of not forgetting your families, friends, and most importantly, not forgetting yourself while striving to achieve your life goals and targets.

In February 2007, I returned to Nagpur to join the company where I am currently employed. However, it wasn't solely for professional reasons; I had a strong desire to stay with my family and live with them. You may need to make a few sacrifices while prioritising your family, but isn't that worth it? Achieving everything at the expense of family and those precious moments doesn't seem like a good deal to me, though this is purely my perspective, and I might be mistaken.

Returning to my experience in Mumbai, when my uncle and aunt would leave us in the care of my aunt's mother, whom we called 'Aaji,' I felt incredibly lonely and isolated. I had grown up in a large family, enjoying summers to the fullest by playing with my siblings, cousins, friends, and other family members. However, in Mumbai, I suddenly found myself missing all those people and cherished moments.

When my uncle invited me to go to Mumbai with him, he promised me lots of excursions, fun, beach visits, movie outings, and much more.

I had high hopes for my stay in Mumbai, but, unfortunately, my expectations didn't come true. I want to emphasise that I'm not blaming my uncle and aunt for this, but rather the way they had chosen to live their lives. Both of them followed a daily routine of waking up at around 6 in the morning, having tea and breakfast, and then rushing to the office, typically by 8 or 8:15. They would return home late, with my aunt getting back around 8 or 8:30 in the evening and my uncle by 9 or 9:30. Their lives seemed incredibly monotonous to me, as if they were living like robots. I must acknowledge that this is just my perception; they might have been content with this lifestyle. However, I was determined not to let my life turn out that way. From that moment onward, I prayed to God to let me be with my family, even if I had work commitments. I believed that while you can spend a day or two, a week or two, or even a month or two away from your family due to work, spending years away and entangled in your work is something I wanted to avoid.

I found myself missing my family, my siblings, my cousins, and the overall environment throughout the day. I managed to cope for about four to five days, but one morning, I woke up crying and my aunt shouted, *"Aho tyala pathaun dya ki"* (Hey, send him back), prompting my aunt to shout at my uncle to make some arrangements to send me back.

My uncle, in response to my aunt's request, questioned, *"Ag pan kunasobat pathau?"* (With whom shall I send him back?)

She replied, *"Bagha, kahitari arrangement kara"* (Just see and make some arrangements), to which my uncle agreed, saying, "OK, let me see."

A few days after this incident, he asked me, "Bala, you want to go. That uncle is going. Will you go with him?"

Without wasting a single minute, I replied, "Yes, uncle."

Finally, I returned to Nagpur with one of our relatives, who was also heading back to Nagpur.

As a child, what did I learn from a particular episode, and more importantly, what did I decide I didn't want from life thereafter? I discovered that I didn't want to become entangled in the demands of work or office life to the extent that they consumed me. Equally, I didn't want to neglect my family and friends, recognising the importance of maintaining meaningful connections. I was adamant about not merely succumbing to the pressures and responsibilities associated with work, or, as I prefer to call it, the tensions that come with it. Moreover, I realized the significance of not losing oneself in the pursuit of success and responsibilities and acknowledged the importance of staying true to one's identity. It's not that I advocate not taking work seriously or setting ambitious life goals; on the contrary, I believe in pursuing such objectives wholeheartedly.

My only request is that before you get overwhelmed by materialistic pursuits, take a moment to consider what truly matters in the long run. While we often plan for financial stability in old age through pensions and savings, it's equally important to value the support of 'human' connections—family, friends, or others. Remember to treasure these relationships alongside your financial endeavours because, in the end, emotional support is just as vital as financial security. Neglecting these connections in youth may lead to regrets in later years of solitude. This is a lesson I've personally found crucial, though I acknowledge others may see it differently. It's October 9, 2010, Saturday night, almost 11:30 p.m. I'm signing off for the night. Goodbye and good night!

The Unforgettable Chapter: The Worst Day Of My Life

Good morning! It's October 10, 2010, Sunday, and I've just woken up, picking up where I left off last night. After my return from Mumbai, I experienced one of the worst days of my life, all due to my own foolishness. Even now, thinking about that incident fills me with deep regret, prompting me to quickly apologise to my mother whenever it crosses my mind.

Let me share the details of this incident. It was during that summer, shortly after my return from Mumbai. On a day filled with games and the carefree enjoyment typical of summer days with no studies or tuition classes, a disagreement arose among my brothers and me. The dispute, related to the game we were playing, escalated quickly, and before we knew it, the matter reached the "Supreme Court" of our household—my mother.

Being a strict woman, she wasted no time in issuing a punishment. We were all confined to a single room for the entire day, with a clear verdict: no food or drink would be provided. Frustrated and angry, especially my cousin, my real brother, and I hatched a plan in that room to teach my mother a lesson the next day.

We were baffled, questioning how our mother could subject us, her children, to being locked up in a room for the entire day. Did she not care about our well-being? However, a mother, as we soon realized, truly cares. After just two or three hours, she entered the room and tried to make us realize our mistakes and that fighting among ourselves wasn't a good thing, only causing harm. She tried to make us understand the importance of unity and harmony. And of course, while doing all this, she pampered us and generously provided a lot of treats she had brought in.

We were so angry with her that we just nodded in agreement without really listening or showing interest in what she was trying to convey. The next day, my real brother, my cousin, and I left home around 9–9:30 a.m. with no intention of returning. We didn't know where to go, what to do, or what the consequences might be—we simply left. Our sole focus was to teach our mother a lesson. We ran about three to four kilometres away, having had enough to satisfy our hunger before leaving. In that radius, we roamed, intending to have fun, instill fear, and teach her a lesson. Unfortunately, this marks the beginning of the worst part—a moment that still fills me with shame and brings tears to my eyes upon recollection.

After about an hour or an hour and a half, around 11–11:30 a.m., we spotted our mother searching for us. Witnessing her panic, we played a game of hide and seek with her. In 10–15 minutes, she disappeared from that spot to search elsewhere, and the game continued. Whenever we saw her, we hid and then followed to observe her reactions. At one point, she spotted us, her eyes lit up, and she yelled, *"Bala, beta thamb, Aai radte"* (Bala, child, please stop, mother's crying). But despite her pleas, we foolishly ran away again.

Not knowing what she was going through or what she was experiencing—trust me, my eyes are numb as I write this. I can still vividly recall her face running towards us, crying, and yelling in a desperate request for us to stop.

This lasted for perhaps an hour or so, and she eventually had no choice but to return home. Not giving up, she returned with a few more people to search for us. This time, my mother, her sister (my aunt), and my elder cousin sister joined in the search. The game continued until around 6:30–7 p.m. in the evening. As the sun started to set and it grew darker, we began feeling a bit scared, wondering what would happen if it got completely dark—where would we go and what would we do?

Eventually, we decided that enough pain had been inflicted, and before things got worse for us, we should go back home. So, we deliberately let my aunt spot us but not my mother. When my aunt approached, she scolded and yelled at us, saying, *"Kay re tumhala mahiti ahe ka aai chi kay halat zaliye? Kiti radtye ti."* (Do you know the state your mother is in? She's just crying.) *"Ani bala tu, beta, tu tar sarvat motha ahe na, tula pan aaichi daya nahi aali?"* (And Bala, you are the eldest; didn't you feel anything for your mother?) These words broke me into pieces.

When we returned with my aunt, all I witnessed was my mother lying on the ground, seemingly half-dead. She hadn't had anything, not even a sip of water, since we went missing. She was just crying, comforted by the other elders in the home. Words can't capture what I felt at that moment. All I can express is a lifelong apology to my mother for causing her that pain.

I don't think there's anyone else on this planet who does everything for you—who lives, dies, cries, laughs for you, and considers you their sole life—except for your parents. But on that day, I disrespected one of them—my mother. I inflicted life-altering pain on her, making it the worst day of my life, with me being the reason. Nothing can be worse than causing pain to those who are the reason for your existence. Mom, I'm sorry for this. Please forgive me.

New School, New Beginning

After completing the seventh grade, as promised by my parents, I was enrolled in another school, approximately double the distance from my previous one. This institution had one of the oldest and largest campuses in the city. There were hardly any CBSE schools in those times. Interestingly, the school's name began with the word 'NEW'. It was June 24th, 1995, a date I recall with certainty, as schools typically opened around this time unless it was a Sunday.

Accompanied by my mother, I approached the school with a sense of happiness and anticipation, eager to experience a newer, bigger, and better educational environment. Along the way, my mind buzzed with questions about the teachers, the students, and what the school would be like.

Upon reaching the school door and attempting to enter the campus, I felt a bit nervous, primarily due to the imposing size of the school buildings. There were four structures on the same campus, each larger than the previous one. Until then, I had attended comparatively smaller schools in Nanded, Warthi, or the earlier one in Nagpur. Moreover, the school timing until seventh grade, wherever I studied, used to be in the morning hours, i.e., by noon, I used to be at home. But here, the school hours had shifted from morning hours to 12 p.m. to 5:30 p.m., meaning I would spend almost the entire day at school.

Fortunately, since it was Saturday and the first day, we were allowed to go home early, with the school session lasting only two to three hours. Most parents, including my mother, waited on campus during this time. When the final bell rang, signaling the end of the day, we all rushed out to head home. I hurried to my mother, and together we began our journey back home.

"Kas vatl, bala? kashi ahe school?" (How did you feel, Bala? How is the school?) asked my mother.

"*Aai, chan ahe, pan thodi nahi jara jastach mothi ahe.*" (Mother, it's good, but it's too big), replied I.

"*Tula avdli na pan.*" (I hope you like it), she asked back.

"*Ho ho nakki*" (yes, surely, I did), I replied, though not entirely from the bottom of my heart.

The next day, she asked, "*Bala ata aaj pasun tu jashil na ekta?*" (Bala, I hope you will go on your own now.) "Of course, mother, I will," I replied.

And I started for the school.

Now, the amusing part is that I would encounter my former school on the way to my new school—it was en route. Every day, as I made my way to the new school, I regularly passed by my previous one. On that particular day, as I started and reached my earlier school, my heart grew a bit heavy. Suddenly, I found myself missing my former school—the four years I had spent there, the friends I had made, the teachers, the environment, and everything about it. However, I had no choice but to continue on to the new school.

So, that day, I arrived at my new school. Now, I had to be there from 12 pm to 5:30 pm, and for me, it felt like a lifetime. Being new to the school campus, I was already nervous, and it became increasingly challenging for me to accept one thing—a question lingered in my mind. Was it I who insisted on changing schools? Because it was me who had fought fiercely with my parents for this change, I had no option but to go to the new school without making much of a drama.

And so, I did. On that second day of school, I somehow managed to endure the entire time—physically present, but mentally still wandering somewhere else.

The next morning, my theatrical performance began.

"Aai pott far dukhatay g," (Mother, my stomach hurts) I complained to her.

"Kay zal re?" (What happened?) she inquired.

"Ag pott dukhtay mhtl na," (I told you, I have stomach pain), I replied assertively.

"Nahi janar ka shalela?" (Won't you go to school?) she asked.

"Ho, nahi Jamel jayala." (Yes, I won't be able to go) I replied while smiling internally.

"Okay, have some rest." She agreed to my plan.

And somehow, I managed to get through that day. However, deep down, I knew that this drama was just a brief appearance, as I had to be regular in school from a certain point onward. And that was troubling me a lot.

Eventually, I decided to do what I had been avoiding until then. Yes, I started running back home from school daily, perhaps after attending just a couple of classes. This became a daily routine—I would run away from school and return home around 2–2:30 pm, often in tears. My mother continually inquired, convinced, and consoled me, even reminding me of how I had fought to change schools.

But I insisted, saying, *"Thik ahe zali mazi chuki,"* (Okay, I made a mistake), but now I want to return to the previous school. She put in all her efforts to make me understand that my behavior was unfair. I told her, *"Aai mala nahi avdat ti shala... maze kunich mitra nahi tithe."* (Mother, I don't like that school. I don't have a single friend there). She comforted me, calming me down and encouraging me to make new friends.

This continued for maybe ten to fifteen days, during which my mother didn't inform my father about the situation. When I remained unconvinced, she finally brought the matter to my father one night.

That night, my father reassured me, saying, *"Bala, ikde ye beta, ikde ye, ghabaru nko; pappa ahe na mi tuza... ikde ye... sang mala; kay zal, ka tu shaletun palun yetos?"* (Bala, come here, come here, child... don't be scared... I am your dad. Please come here. Tell me, what happened? Why did you come back home, leaving school in between?) A bit scared, I replied, *"Pappa, mala nahi avdt ti shala. Far mothi ahe... mitra pan nahit kuni."* (Dad, I don't like that school. It's too big, and I don't have any friends there.)

My father comforted me, saying, *"Arey beta, roj jashil, bolshil, abhays karshil, tar nave mitra bantil ki."* (You will go to school every day, talk to others, study, and make new friends.)

Being a father, he too made sincere efforts to make me comfortable and understand why I shouldn't continue my actions.

"Mag jashil na udya pasun roj shalet," (So, will you go to school daily from tomorrow?) he asked, summing up his advice to me.

"Yes, dad," I replied, sounding very low and unconfident.

The next day, I repeated the same story, running back home within an hour or so. Now, it was becoming increasingly challenging for my parents to tolerate my daily drama, especially when there seemed to be no valid reason for it.

On one fateful day, the volcano finally erupted. My father, typically the calmest and coolest person I had ever seen, erupted like never before. It had been almost fifteen to twenty days of my recurring drama, and that day, I faced the music from him, an unforgettable moment in my life.

Eventually, he turned to my mother and said, *"Ghe tuze lad ahe... tula mhtl hot nko aiku tyach... kahi garaz nahi nav kadhayachi... tayla kay kalt... ata ghya... mi leaving certificate chi application lihun deto... nav kadh tyach... ani basav ghari... kara doghehi kay karayach te... ani mala maf kara."* (See, it's your pampering and overcare. I had warned you. Don't listen to him. There was no need to change the school. What does he understand? Pay the price now. I am writing an application for a leaving certificate. Get him off the school and ask him to sit at home. Do what both of you want to. But please forgive me).

And then, he left. Then there was all that crying—this time, not me, but my mother.

I went to her and said, *"Aai, tu ka radtes... mazyamule pappa tula ragavale... mhanun na?"* (Mother, why are you crying? Did father get angry with you because of me?)

"Nahi re Bala," (No, my child), she said, cuddling me. But I could see she was paying the price for my mistake.

"Aai, mi udyapsun roj zail shalet... mazyamule tula trass nahi hou denar. Pappa khup ragavale na tula, udyapsun nahi ragavnar." (Mother, I will go to school regularly starting tomorrow. I won't let you suffer because of me. Dad yelled at you. I promise it won't happen tomorrow," I said, wiping her tears.

She just smiled, saying nothing, and cuddled me tightly. The next day, with a firm resolution not to let my mother face my dad's anger because of me, I started school. I sat for the entire day, attending all the classes, though with some anxiety, nervousness, and restlessness. Needless to mention, she was there in school too until 5:30 p.m.— yes, my mother. I'm feeling emotional as I write this. That day, after 5:30 p.m., when the school was over, I ran back to my mother, who was patiently waiting for my school hours to get over at the administrative block. I saw a world of happiness and satisfaction on her face.

She was so happy to see me complete my school hours without making any drama. Really, she was happy, and so was I. When we came back home, it felt like I had conquered the entire world.

That night, when my father returned home from the office, my mother wasted no time in sharing the news, saying, *"Aaj aplya balane purn shala keli... palun nahi aala."* (Our Bala did attend the complete school today; he didn't run back home). I could see how pleased she was while narrating this to my father, justifying the decision she had made for me.

My father responded, *"Thik ahe, baghu kiti diwas jato."* (Okay, let's see how long he goes). Trust me, I proved my father wrong and my mother very right. After that day, even today, I don't remember a single day of me running back home between school hours because I never did so.

A Dream Came True

Thus, a new beginning started with a new school, a dream came true. My new school life began, and as I mentioned, I never let my mother down, going to school regularly, bringing happiness to my parents.

After a couple of months, I approached my mother and said, *"Aai, shalet jatana na khup payi chalav lagt mala cycle gheun deshil ka?"* (Mother, I need to walk a lot to go to school; will you please buy a bicycle for me?).

Although I knew, by this time, the economic condition we had wasn't that bad, I understood that additional expenses like a bicycle would burden my father. While he earned enough to fulfill the basic needs of the entire family and provide support to my two uncles, any extra expenses would be challenging for him, as I could gather from discussions between my parents.

Even though it wasn't fair to ask my mother for a bicycle, I still made the request.

"Pappa na yeu de, sayankali bolu tyanchyashi," (Let Dad come; we'll talk to him in the evening), replied my mother.

"Pan aai tu pappa na manvashil na?" (But mother, will you make Dad agree for this?) asked I curiously.

"Bala, beta khar bolu ka, agodarch far kharch ahe... tumha tighancha shalecha Kharch, gharacha kharch, baki pan kharch ahet na, mala thod kathin vattey... tari pan bolun baghil pappa shi... baghu kay mhantat te?" (Child, look, there are already so many expenses—school expenses for all three of you, other household expenses—I think it's difficult. But still, I will talk to Dad; let's see what he says), explained my mother.

"Thik ahe aai, mi jast hatta hai karnar pappan kade... pan tu fakt ekda bolun baghshil," (Okay, Mother, I won't force Dad, but still, you at least have

a word), said I, in agreement with her, though not so willingly and with a heavy heart.

"*Chalel*," (Okay) she said, smiling.

That evening, I was desperately waiting for my father to come back home, but you know, when you need something very badly and when you dream of something impatiently, he, yes, almighty, tests your patience even harder. And the same was the case with me; I had been waiting for my father to come, but that day he didn't come at his usual time, which used to be around 7.30–8 p.m. However, I was very firm and determined not to go to bed unless I, along with my mother, spoke to him about the bicycle. Eventually, somewhere around 9.30–10, he came back.

He was already upset from the challenges he faced at the office that day, and his frustration was evident. As he freshened up and sat down for dinner, I entered the kitchen. Typically, he would dine in the kitchen, with my mother serving him, and I would join him, following our routine of sharing a meal. However, on that particular day, I found myself unusually silent.

"*Kay re kay zal, ka chup aaj ekdum.*" (What happened, why are you quiet today?) my father inquired.

"*Pay dukhtat ahet tyache,*" (He has leg pain), my mother promptly responded.

"*Ka kay zal, khup dhawala, khelala ka?*" (What happened? Did he run, play too much?) he asked.

"No, he has to walk a lot while going to and coming back from school," my mother explained.

I silently listened to the conversation, curious about whether my mother would succeed in convincing Dad about getting a bicycle. I prayed to God to grant my wish.

And... I Met Myself

"Ha mag kay mhanan ahe tyach, kay karayach?" (So, what does he say then? What to do?) my father inquired in response to my mother's explanation.

"kahi nahi, mi mhante tyala ek cycle gheun deu ya," (Nothing, I think we must buy him a bicycle) replied my mother.

"Dok firl ka? Kiti traffic ahe rastyane; ani as kiti dur ahe shalla tyachi," (Are you out of your mind? There is heavy traffic on that road and, by the way, how far is his school?) my father exclaimed, raising his pitch.

"Tyachya faltu goshti aiakat nko jaau......ani tasahi sadhya budget nahi.... baghu nanter," (Don't listen to his nonsense, anyway, there is no budget for that now; let's see later) he explained, this time more softly.

"Kay re, Bala, khupach jaroori ahe ka cycle aatach agdi?" (Bala, is a bicycle a must now?) he questioned.

"Nahi, pappa, nanter baghuya," (No Dad, let's see sometime later) replied I, again not willingly and a bit apprehensively.

"Good boy, go play with your siblings for a while and then head to bed," he said.

"Yes, Dad," I replied and hurried away. The next day, as usual, Dad left for the office around 8:30-9 in the morning, and by 11-11:15, I began preparing for school.

"Kay re naraz ahes ak, pappani cycle sathi nahi mhtl mhanun?" (Are you upset, Bala? Because Dad said no to the bicycle.) asked my mother.

I smiled a bit and replied, *"Nahi g, Aai; mulich nahi."* (No, Mom, not at all.)

"Shahana ahe baal maza," (You're quite wise, my child), she praised. Recalling all this is making me smile again.

"Chal Aai jato," (I'm going, Mom.) I said, leaving for school. Little did I know that a surprise awaited me that day.

When I returned home, my mother approached me and asked, *"Kay aaj pay nahi dukhat ahet naa?"* (Is there no leg pain today?)

"Nahi, Aai, nahi," (No, Mom, none) I replied.

"Aik, Bala, mi mavashi kade geli hoti... dada chi cycle ahe thodi sudhravawi lagel pan chan ahe, anayachi ti? chalto aata baghayala?" (Listen, Bala, I visited your aunt today. Your cousin's bicycle is in fairly good condition—it needs some repair, but it's still good. Shall we bring it? Shall we go take a look?) asked my mother.

"Ho, Aai chal aatach jauya baghayala," (Sure, Mom, let's go check it out right away) I said with immense joy on my face. We headed to my aunt's place, conveniently located within walking distance from our home. They had a better economic standing than us, and my aunt had purchased a bicycle for her son about 6-7 years ago.

Upon reaching my aunt's place, I promptly asked her, *"Mavashi kuthe ahe g cycle?"* (Aunt, where's the bicycle?)

"Arey ti var adgalit thevliye," (Oh, it's kept upstairs in a storage room) she replied.

I rushed upstairs, but truth be told, I had a mixed reaction when I laid eyes on that bicycle. It was covered in dust, its chain and sprocket had separated, the bell on its handle was missing, leaving only the bell clamp behind, and the rubber cushion on one of the handle arm grips was gone. The paint had flaked off in several areas, not to mention the seat was missing, revealing only the rod where it is normally attached.

"Kashi ahe...chan ahe na?" (How is it? Isn't it good?) asked my mother.

"*Ho aai chan ahe,*" (Yes, mother, it's good) I replied, though I don't know how that 'Yes' came out of my mouth.

"*Zal tar mag, dada ala ki mavshi sangel tyala sudharvayala takayala, ekdum navin houn jail mag ti,*" (Alright then, let's wait for brother (referring aunt's son) to come. Aunt will ask him to give it for repair, and it will be completely new) said my mother excitedly.

"Okay," I replied, equally nonchalant.

That evening, my mother informed my dad, "*Aho aika, Ashish chi cycle sangitlieye repair karayala.*" (Hey, listen, I've asked for Ashish's (referring to aunt's son) bicycle to be repaired.)

"*Ok....kiti kharch sangitla*" (Okay, what's the expected cost of repair?) he asked.

"*Maya baghel, tich boli tass, nanter deun deuya aapan,*" (Maya (my aunt) will take care of it; she said we can pay her later), said my mother.

"*Hmm, thik ahe,*" (Hmm, okay) said my dad, not so convincingly.

I, not particularly interested as it was a second-hand and unattractive bicycle, listened to the conversation without much enthusiasm. None of us, my dad and I, took the matter seriously, except for my mother, who was quite excited.

A few days later, "*Bala, aaj dada dupari cycle anun denar ahe, kal mavashi kade geli hoti tevha bolala to zali mhane purn pane sudharavun.*" (Bala, brother's going to bring the bicycle by noon. Yesterday I had been to your aunt, where he told me that it's completely repaired now) said my mother as I was getting ready for school.

I just smiled at her and said, "Okay."

I could see how happy and ecstatic my mother was, and I can still recall her joyful face, a moment I'll never forget.

When I got back home that day, my mother excitedly told me, "The bicycle has arrived; it's in the backyard." When I say backyard, it's not the backyard of our home; as I already mentioned, it was a very small house. Here, by backyard, I am referring to the public place or area at the rear of our house.

Without wasting time, I rushed to the backyard where it was kept. A silver-colored, swanky, and elegant bicycle, looking brand new, awaited someone to ride it. It was completely cleaned with no dust, the chain and sprocket were restored, the bell was back, the seat and rubber cushion of the handle grip were in place, and it was freshly repainted with no flaking.

The only visible flaw was a welded joint on the bottom of the middle triangular anchor frame, but it didn't detract much from the overall makeover. Despite being painted, it was still noticeable. Otherwise, I couldn't relate it to the outdated piece I had seen at my aunt's house a week ago.

Trust me, my joy knew no bounds the moment I saw that bicycle. I was all smiles within myself. I ran back to my mother, who was eagerly waiting for my reaction and hugged her.

"Aai tu kiti chan ahes," (Mother, you are too good) I said happily.

Mom said, *"Chal chal aata udyapasn gheun jaa cycle shalet."* (Okay, from tomorrow take this bicycle.)

I replied, *"Ho nakki."* (Yes, absolutely)

I asked, *"Aai pappa kay mhantil g?"* (Mother, what would Dad say?)

She said, *"Baghu aata."* (Let's see)

Up until that point, I had always seen a school kid in a television advertisement riding a bicycle singing, *School time... Action ka school time.*

My dream of having a bicycle to go to school came true that day, and I was ecstatic.

Luckily, or perhaps it was destined, Dad came back home early around 6 pm that day and saw me all smiling, playing, and happy. He asked, *"kay re, kay zal? far khush ahes."* (Hey, what happened? You look very happy)

I replied, *"Pappa cycle aliye."* (Dad, the bicycle has come)

He glanced at my mother, undoubtedly with a few questions in his mind. I could sense it was related to the expenses incurred in repairing and renovating the bicycle. Eventually, he had to plan how to pay it back to my aunt. However, my mom simply responded with a smile, conveying everything without uttering a single word, just blinking her eyes and offering a mild smile. He was convinced, and so was I. We were all happy. I could see my mom with a sense of satisfaction, knowing she had put in all her efforts to win the hearts of both me and my dad. I was excited about getting a new bicycle, and my dad was grateful for my mom's efforts in managing the entire process for the sake of their child. She did so without immediately burdening her husband, although he did eventually pay it back to my aunt.

Yes, she had succeeded in it. And as the caption says, my dream had come true.

When Something Goes Wrong, It's Followed By Something Good

As I settled into my new school routine, I gradually became familiar with the campus and the overall environment. Over time, I made new friends, and I found myself truly enjoying my experience in the new school.

However, there were certain challenges in my studies. Transitioning from a Marathi medium school to a lower English medium school meant that science and mathematics were now taught in English, which was different from what I had studied in all my previous schools. The first word that became a source of frustration for me was "PERPENDICULAR." Every encounter with this word annoyed me, and I couldn't help but think, "Couldn't they choose a better and easier word...?"

As the academic year approached its end, I found myself anxious about whether I would pass the examination and progress to the next class. Adding to my worries was a girl who stayed nearby and to whom I went for private tuition. Her family was education-focused and literate, unlike ours. Since I was in a lower English medium, my mother thought it would be beneficial for me to study with her.

By the time I reached the eighth standard, the girl, referred to as Didi, was in the twelfth standard and had faced challenges in clearing her tenth board examination. My mother would often remind me of Didi's struggles, saying, "Bala, look, she knows how hard it is. She had a tough time clearing the tenth board examination. You need to study hard." I would reassure her, saying, "Yes, don't worry, please."

Despite my assurances, there was an underlying nervousness as the pressure to perform well in the examination weighed on me. Now, turning back to the title of this portion, everything narrated so far under this heading has no relevance to it. The real story about this caption starts here.

As mentioned earlier, I began attending school regularly and thoroughly enjoyed my time at the new school. I would ride my bicycle to school, and with this new mode of transportation, I altered my route to avoid passing by my previous school, which I used to encounter before I had the bicycle. Instead, I preferred a wider main road over the smaller lanes.

However, one day, around January 1996, as I was about to leave for school, I discovered that both tires of my bicycle were punctured. It became clear that this was an intentional act by mischievous individuals in the area. I informed my mother that I would walk to school that day but requested that she ensure the tires were repaired by the time I returned home. "Ok," she agreed, and I set out for school on foot.

It had been almost five to six months since I had taken the previous route due to the change caused by the bicycle. Curious and nostalgic, I decided to take the old route, the one I used before having the bicycle. My primary motivation was the chance to see my friends, particularly one—childhood crush.

By this point, I was fully integrated into the new environment of the school and had made new friends. The probability of encountering my old friends, including the childhood crush, was almost zero. I would have merely passed by the campus without actually going inside the school to meet them. But still with that dormant wish, I took that route.

Trust me, what I witnessed next felt nothing short of miraculous. The joy was immense because I had a wish, the probability of which was almost nil, and suddenly, it happened—my wish came true. Isn't that a miracle?

As I approached the school with this dormant wish, my eyes suddenly lit up with joy. To my surprise, both childhood crush and her companion—someone who always accompanied her—emerged from the school doors. Perhaps, they stayed close to the school and went home during break; the reason was unclear. I made eye contact with both of them.

In a non-verbal exchange, they smiled at me, questioning with their eyes if I was the one who had studied with them till the seventh grade. Without wasting any time, I responded with a simple blink of my eyes, affirming and smiling. The entire interaction happened within a fraction of a minute without any verbal communication. None of us spoke, none of us stopped walking. It all unfolded as we continued walking.

I cannot speak for them, but I had a warm feeling that I still cherish, for reasons unknown. The joy I experienced stemmed from the simple recognition and acknowledgment they gave me with their smiles. It's worth noting that both of them were the top two studious students in the school. Despite any jealousy I may have felt towards their academic weightage and family background, I harbored no grudges. It was a moment of joy for me, and I continued on my way, all smiles.

Now, let's connect this to the title of this section. As I mentioned earlier, when I discovered my bicycle was punctured just before leaving for school, frustration overtook me, and I started cursing the moment. However, this inconvenience led me to walk to school, prompting me to take an alternate route with a dormant wish that seemed improbable to come true.

To my surprise, fate seemed to favour me, and the improbable wish did come true when I unexpectedly encountered childhood crush and her companion. However, the story doesn't conclude there. While I walked away happily after meeting them, my mind became flooded with thoughts.

Numerous questions lingered in my mind like, What if I didn't pass my eighth class? I would be left behind, while the duo, childhood crush and her companion, moved forward. What would everyone think—both of them and my former schoolmates—should they discover I failed the examination? What would my family think? These thoughts compelled me to take a serious and focused approach to my studies, determined to clear the examination at any cost.

And thus started, my extra efforts to clear the examination.

This time around, my focus wasn't on achieving a high percentage but on simply clearing the examination and avoiding failure at all costs. I took the exam, and by the time it concluded, I was confident that I had succeeded.

When the results were announced, not only had I passed the examination, but my class had gained one more studious individual. Looking back at this episode and relating it to the caption—bicycle getting punctured, something that went wrong—I decided to walk to school with an alternate route, leading to an unexpected encounter with those two girls along the way. This encounter made me more attentive and focused on my studies, driven by an inherent and self-decided competition I had with them. Eventually, I performed well in the examination, and something good followed.

So, the lesson is not to lose faith in the almighty because something may go wrong, only to be followed by something good.

A Woman—A Mother, A Sister, A Wife, A Teacher, And What Not?

How can I forget that day? It was after the eighth standard, around September-October 1996, on a Saturday. Since it was a Saturday, our school hours were in the morning. Heavy rain on the previous day, Friday, and a prediction of continued rain on Saturday led me to decide to skip school. As I was not well for the past few days, I had already decided on Friday to skip the school on Saturday. However, on Saturday morning, as the rain dramatically subsided, I changed my mind and decided to go, against my mother's wishes. Despite her convincing me not to go due to my recent illness, I eventually left for school.

By the time I reached school, the rain had completely stopped. The school decided to conduct the morning prayer and National Anthem on the ground, which would normally be done in the classroom if the weather was unfavorable. We gathered for the morning prayer and National Anthem.

Due to my recent illness, where I had been surviving on juices, doctor-prescribed supplements, and occasional biscuits, my strength was drained, and I felt very weak. I wasn't in the mood to go to the ground and attend the prayer, but I joined my classmates, ignoring my poor health.

As we gathered on the ground, queuing up, the prayer began. Due to my weakened state, it started getting darker in front of my eyes. I fainted, collapsing on the ground. Before losing consciousness, I remember desperately trying to grab onto the person standing ahead of me in the queue, but my efforts were in vain.

I was unconscious, but I could feel a couple of classmates holding me and carrying me to the restroom in the school. When I regained consciousness, perhaps half an hour later, I found myself resting in a room. My shoes had been taken off, and my belt was loosened at the waist. Our class teacher was gently rubbing my soles to comfort me.

"What happened, Akhil?" she asked, sitting by my side throughout that half-hour until I fully recovered.

"Nothing, ma'am. I haven't been keeping well for the last two or three days," I replied.

"Child, then you should not have come to school," she advised.

"Hmm," I responded, shaking my head.

"Ganesh beta, pani aan hyachyakarita," (Ganesh, please bring a glass of water for him) she instructed an office boy who was nearby.

"kahi khashil ka?" (Will you have something?) She asked me.

"No, ma'am, I am all right now," I replied.

Trust me, she cared for me as if she were my mother. I was overwhelmed by the way she looked after me. I could see the concern in her eyes for a child whose parents were not around while he was sick and down.

It was challenging for me to understand why she was so concerned for me, just a student. Regardless, I appreciated all the warmth and care she extended to me, making me feel as if I were being taken care of by my mother.

"Ghari janar vyavasthit, ki kunala sodayala sangu?" (Are you going home on your own, or shall I ask someone to drop you home?) she asked.

"No, ma'am, I will go," I replied.

"Nako nako asuch de, sangte mi kunala tuzya sobat jayala," (No, no, I'll arrange for someone to accompany you) she insisted.

"Okay, ma'am," I agreed.

Finally, two of my friends accompanied me on the way back home, as per our teacher's instructions.

"Kar re lavkar alas? Kay zal?" (Why did you come home early? What happened?) my mother inquired when I arrived.

"Kaku, to chakkar yeun padla shalet," (Aunty, he fainted down in school) yelled both of my friends who had accompanied me.

"Arey baba, kay zal re? Lagl vagere tar nahi na padlyamule?" (Oh my God, what happened? Were you injured? Did you fall on the ground?) my concerned mother asked.

"No, mom, I am all right," I reassured her.

"Ja re tumhi, ghari ja, thik ahe mi aata," (You can go home now; I am fine) I told my friends.

"Kay re Bala, tula bolli na mi agodarch, barr nahiye, nko jaus," (Bala, I had already told you not to go if you weren't well) scolded my mother, cuddling me.

"You don't listen to me," she continued.

"I'm sorry, Mom," I apologized with a smile.

"Mom, can I ask you something?" I queried.

"Yes, go ahead," she replied.

"Are women too emotional?" I asked.

"Why? What happened? Why are you asking this?" she inquired with a smile.

And I narrated the entire episode that had happened in school and how the class teacher cared for me like a mother.

Smiling, my mother explained, "It's not that women are too emotional, but every woman carries the heart of a mother inside her. When she sees someone in a state of discomfort, distress, and uneasiness, the mother inside her gets restless, and she tries to do what she can to see him happy, to relieve him of that pain. It hardly matters who he is; she just sees her child in that person and without a second thought, she moves forward to help him."

"Mhanunach tar Bala, Samarth Ramdas Swami mhantat, 'Swami tinhi jagacha, aai vina bhikari'" (That's why Ramdas Swami says, 'Even the Lord, the Almighty, is poor without a mother)' she added, just cuddling me.

"Understood, child?" she asked.

"Yes, Mom, I got it," I replied, all smiles.

"Bala, remember one thing—never disrespect or dishonor a woman, don't talk unkind to her. How would you feel if someone disrespects me? Please, keep this in mind," said my mother, holding both of my hands.

"Aani aai mansanna?" (And what about men?) I asked, inquisitively.

"Arey murkha, kunachach anadar nahi karayacha, mansancha pan nahi," (Silly boy, don't disrespect anyone, not even men) she explained, gently squeezing my ear with love.

"Ho aai, kalal," (Yes, Mom, understood) I replied.

Ever since then, women have held a special place for me. That episode of my teacher caring for me like a mother and the subsequent wisdom my mother gave me really elevated a woman's stature in my eyes. Truly, what doesn't a woman do? She keeps her child in her womb for nine months, and the child breathes through her, lives through her, sees the world through her, and then comes to this beautiful world, of course, through her. We can't deny, we are indebted to a woman.

And I Paid For Someone Else's Mistake

Before I share anything under this heading, a song by the legendary singer Yesudas comes to mind. It's *"Teri choti si ek bhul ne sara gulshan zala diya,"* (The small mistake of yours has ruined the entire garden) specifically one line in that song, *"Jane na kaha ki rit hai ye, koi kare aur koi bhare... nyay nahi anyay hai ye, doshi jiye nirdosh mare."* (Do not know where this tradition comes from, one does and the other bears... It's not justice, it's injustice, the guilty lives, and the innocent dies) On a lighter note, even today, I don't know what mistake I made for which I had to pay that day.

In December 1997, one of my friends asked me to accompany him to the teacher's room. To provide some background on this friend, he had lost his father during childhood, and his mother ran a small business selling daily necessities like milk, bread, and newspapers. She didn't have a shop but would set up a stand near our school to sell these items. Doorstep services were not common at that time, except for newspapers and, occasionally, milk in specific areas. We would typically go to specific places or shops to purchase these daily necessities, as the availability of daily need centers, shops, or dairies was limited. My friend supplied milk to our school, making him well-known among the school staff.

On that particular day, he asked me to accompany him to the teacher's room, where teachers kept their belongings and spent spare time between classes. As we approached the room, I suggested that he go inside and complete his task, assuring him that I would wait at the room entrance. While he entered the room, I stood at the door, patiently waiting for him to finish.

Inside, a group of teachers engaged in conversation around a round table. An older teacher, whose name I can't recall, rather I don't want to quote, suddenly stared at me for reasons unknown. He gestured for me to come to him, and in a state of confusion about why he was calling me, I followed his signal. When I reached him, he didn't utter a single word, nor did he ask any questions. Instead, he instructed me to bend down slightly. Anticipating a question, I complied, only to receive a sudden and unexpected slap.

Confused and bewildered, I asked, "Sir, what happened? Why did you slap me?"

His face flushed with anger, he ordered me to leave without providing an explanation for the slap. Despite repeatedly asking, I received no answers, and eventually, under the threat of severe consequences, I reluctantly left.

However, the humiliation lingered, and I couldn't easily shake it off. When my friend returned and inquired about the incident, my fury intensified. The thought of a teacher treating me this way consumed me. He laughed and proceeded to clarify the reason behind the teacher's actions.

According to my friend, a fellow student from our class, who typically accompanied him and was a regular visitor to the teacher's room, had verbally abused the teacher a few days earlier. This particular teacher, known for being strict and unfriendly, had a strained relationship with students. They often tried to avoid him due to his demeanor.

On that fateful day, as the teacher rode his two-wheeler home, the same student took advantage of the situation and hurled abusive language at him. The teacher, not clearly seeing the student but noticing my friend instead, might have later learned about the student's usual association with my friend.

Unfortunately, on the day the teacher was ready to explode, I had accompanied my friend to the teacher's room instead of the student who had verbally abused him. The result was the unexpected slap that I had received.

By the time my friend explained the situation to me, I had calmed down and understood the teacher's likely state of mind during the incident, considering his age. However, the episode didn't end there. As I returned to my class and shared the story with other close friends, various speculations arose. One student claimed the teacher had a conflict with a man on his way to school that day, carrying the anger into the classroom. Another suggested that someone had punctured the teacher's bike, and, not knowing the culprit, he took out his frustration on me. Numerous stories circulated, each offering a different perspective on the teacher's actions.

By this point, my annoyance had completely subsided, and we were all able to look back on the incident with smiles. I had come to the realization that I had paid the price for someone else's mistake. However, a lingering question remained in the back of my mind, even to this day: Why had he slapped me? I can't help but smile at the irony of the situation.

A Parallel Student Life At A Private Tuition Class

In addition to my life as a student in school, there was a parallel student life at a private coaching class. Let me share how I ended up joining that coaching class.

After I enrolled in the new school, where I had opted for lower English medium, my mother became concerned about whether I could cope with the studies. The science subjects and mathematics were now being taught in English, a shift from Marathi.

"Bala, will you be able to handle this through English Medium? Shall we have tuition for you?" asked my mother soon after I started going to school regularly.

"No, there is no need… I will manage," replied I. However, my mother, concerned about our studies, consulted our neighbor, whose elder daughter excelled in studies with a higher English medium.

That evening, she informed me, *"Bala, mi vicharpus keliye… javalach ahe tuze classes… don week nanter suru honar."* (Bala, I have enquired… the tuition classes are just within walking distance… and will commence after two weeks.)

"Ok, Mom," I replied. And so, my life at the private tuition class was about to begin. It didn't start that year, though, due to a delay in commencement and my mother's short-tempered nature. Frustrated with the delayed start, my mother canceled my admission and received a refund.

I was delighted as I didn't want to attend that class and preferred going to the girl, 'a Didi,' mentioned earlier, who was senior to me. So, I didn't attend any professional tuition classes while in eighth grade.

However, the next year, my mother revisited the same coaching class to ensure it would commence on the given date. It did, marking the beginning of another student's life at this coaching class.

So, by the time, a couple of months passed by, I was quite famous amongst the students and of course in the eyes of my tuition teacher as well, not because of my study performance, but because of my mother, as a typical 'mama's boy'.

Because of my mother's visits, the teacher knew me well. Regular updates about my studies and progress from the tuition teacher made me somewhat famous among students and the tuition teacher. Over the first couple of months, my mother's occasional visits provided me with eye-openers in front of the entire crowd whenever the teacher complained about my study performance.

It was a challenging day for me, perhaps three or four months into the coaching class when my mother unexpectedly visited while the session was ongoing. She approached my teacher to inquire about my progress, and I'm unsure about what he communicated to her. However, her reaction was unmistakable – she slapped me in front of the entire class, loudly scolding, "You nonsense, why don't you study properly?"

The embarrassing moment wasn't solely due to the fact that my mother had slapped me but rather because it happened in front of the entire class. Let me provide some context about the class itself. The coaching class was located in the vicinity of the Gujrati, Marwari, Sindhi communities. Most students joining were from these communities, holding advantages in terms of economic background, liberal family background, academic talent, and everyday business knowledge. This created an upper edge for non-Marathi students compared to the introverted, less economically privileged Marathi students, except for a few with exceptional talents.

This incident would have further isolated a Marathi student, reinforcing the tendency to stay within a shell. The day left me feeling so down that I couldn't focus on the class or studies after my mother's departure, only getting a glimpse of the potential consequences I might face in the days to come if I didn't improve my academic performance.

I remained silent and spoke to nobody that day until the class was over and I returned home. However, it was only after the mid-year examinations, just before Diwali, that I stood at the top of the class. By this time, the entire class knew about the new, shy student who excelled in studies.

My tuition teacher was aware of my academic capabilities, but he wanted me to demonstrate it through performance since I tended to be introverted. When the examination results were declared, he was pleased for me, but perhaps more for himself. He knew he would receive appreciation from my mother, ensuring positive publicity for his class – a strategy he had become well-versed in due to his understanding of her nature. Thus began my parallel student life at the private coaching class, where I was acknowledged as one of the studious fellows in the class.

As mentioned earlier in this chapter, most students in the class came from Hindi families, unlike me, who hailed from a typical lower-middle-class Maharashtrian family. This contrast could be seen through their attire, overall appearance, and the way they carried themselves. Consequently, I often felt inferior to them, particularly the non-Marathi students, including girls. However, after the initial six months, I managed to develop a good rapport with both boys and girls in the class.

Recalling a specific incident that made me feel low and triggered memories of childhood crush, it happened around December 1997 or January 1998, on Sankatahara Chaturthi day. This day, dedicated to the Hindu God Ganesh, occurred every lunar month. During the 'Sankatahara Chaturthi', we conducted 'Ganesh Pooja' at home, offering a coconut and twenty-one 'Modaka', a sweet which we made from five to six 'Pedha' (milk fudge).

On that day, my father asked me to go and buy 'Pedha' and a coconut. During that time, we used to walk around half a kilometer to a renowned sweet shop in the area. I bought 'Pedha' from the sweet shop and proceeded to the grocery store, that was opposite it, to purchase a coconut. While waiting for the shopkeeper to return my change, I noticed a girl from my tuition class, one of the most beautiful girls in the class, coming out from the house adjacent to the shop.

We made eye contact and exchanged smiles. Beyond the interaction, I found myself concerned about my appearance—was I dressed appropriately, or did I look funny? I was wearing a half pants and a very old T-shirt, adding to my self-consciousness at that moment.

"How are you here?" she asked.

"I just came to buy this coconut," I replied timidly, lacking confidence.

It didn't take long for me to realize that she quickly noticed my discomfort in being seen in such attire by her. To describe her, as mentioned earlier, she was one of the most beautiful girls in the class, with an added charm of a mole on her chin, much like actress Aruna Irani.

Hold on, don't misinterpret. I was not attracted to that girl, nor did I take her as seriously as the other boys in the class who dreamed of talking to her. For me, she was one of the good-looking and appealing girls in the class. However, at that moment, she reminded me of the childhood crush, and with a smile within myself, I walked away.

Thus, living two lives, or rather two parallel student lives, everything was going smoothly with not much tension about the future and no specific career goal in mind. I moved on and passed my ninth standard. I was enjoying the attention, admiration, and accolades I received at both places—school and the private coaching class.

By the end of the ninth standard, I was more popular in the tuition class than in school, fulfilling my dormant wish. The reason, as mentioned earlier, was the composition of students. In school, most students came from a typical middle-class Maharashtrian family. In the tuition class, the scenario was entirely different, with the majority coming from Hindi families. I aimed to make a mark among them and had succeeded to some extent, albeit in academic achievements only during that phase of my life.

To narrate an incident about the popularity I gained as a gentle, mild, and studious fellow who was a bit introverted, I remember a day with a placid smile.

After passing the ninth standard, our summer study classes for the tenth standard were about to commence in a month. As the ninth standard examinations were over, the tuition teacher decided to have a small gathering, marking a send-off to the tenth standard students and a welcome to us entering the tenth standard.

It was around March-April 1997. On that day, we all gathered in the tuition class for the small get-together early in the morning, around 9 a.m. The front-line players, both male and female students, were busy decorating the class for the celebration later that day. Ninth-passed students, like me, were running here and there, while the tenth-passed students were asked to come a bit later, around 12 p.m.

Being an introverted and shy person, I sat in a corner, observing all that was happening. Suddenly, to my surprise and everyone else's, the same girl I mentioned earlier exclaimed, "Hey, what are you doing here? Are you getting bored? Come with me. We need to buy something. Come on, I won't drop you off the bike. Are you shy to come with me?"

She had offered me to accompany her on her moped bike to buy certain decorative items. Everyone present was awestruck, especially the boys, as none had anticipated that she would offer me to go with her. While for any other boy, it might have felt like winning a million-dollar lottery ticket, for me, I felt good. However, she accurately guessed that I was shy about going with her, as I didn't even move an inch to show any interest or agreement. I simply smiled at her and the other girls who were present.

"Ok, no issues," she said quite casually and walked away.

Before you jump to any judgment, let me clarify that it was very casual and light-hearted incident. She asked with ease, and I denied with the same ease. There were no hiccups from either side. However, for others, it became a topic for light-hearted talk and gossip.

For me, it was a moment that certified my special place in that class. As she walked away, almost everyone came to me and started teasing me, albeit in a positive and playful manner. I was elated and blushing.

That day, I enjoyed every moment, doing nothing but reminiscing about the incident and feeling happy, smiling within myself, thinking, 'Yes, I hold a distinct place; that's why she offered me, leaving all others.'

A Thousand Rupee Worth Of Tension

As I mentioned, our summer study camp for the tenth standard was about to commence, and our tuition teacher had requested a fee of thousand rupees for the two-month session. When he announced the fees, I became nervous, thinking about where my Dad would find the money for this course. It was essentially an act of overthinking on my part, but I genuinely stressed over the idea that these thousand rupees would disturb my father's budget for those two months.

That day, I went home and asked my mother about the fees with a tense voice. *"Aai papa kuthun aantil g paise?"* (Mom, from where will Dad get this money?)

She smiled at me and said, *"Tu ka kalji kartos, bala; papa deil ki."* (Don't worry, your Dad will manage)

I then raised concerns about my sister and brother needing money for their education as well.

"Bala tu khup vichar kartos," (Bala, you overthink) she reassured me. *"Tu fakt Abhyasat laksh de."* (You just focus on your studies)

I replied, *"Ho Aai."* (Yes, Mom)

However, the thought of the financial burden of a thousand rupees on my father continued to weigh heavily on my mind.

Educational Session 1997-1998

I want to emphasize this title precisely because this was the session when I was in the tenth grade. Everyone in the family was focused on me, hoping I would do well in the board examination. My mother and uncle wished for me to pursue science to become a doctor, while my father hoped I would go for civil services. However, I had no clear focus, enjoying life as it came. With no specific aim or target, my only goal was to overcome the poverty we faced, so I was committed to performing well in the examinations.

I completed the summer study camp and then started the regular sessions at both school and the tuition class. I was never the type to burn the midnight oil for studying, although I was good academically. I never took studying too seriously or engaged in late-night study sessions.

As the educational session approached its completion, the board examinations loomed ahead. I felt a bit nervous, understanding that I had to meet the expectations of my parents, siblings, uncle, and other close relatives. However, the realization of my father's sacrifices for our education boosted my confidence to perform well in the examinations.

I eventually took the exams and eagerly awaited the results. The summer vacation began, and the summer of 1998 holds a special place in my memory as it introduced a person into my life to whom I owe everything—a person who will remain significant for the rest of my life.

During the summer vacation, I was keen on enjoying every moment, feeling liberated after a year of intense studying. I had no desire for books or studies; I just wanted to play, explore, and have fun. I aimed to live the moments I missed while dedicated to my academic sessions.

Most of the time during the academic year, when I saw my brothers and friends going out to play, my mother would assure me that it was just a matter of a year, and after my board examinations, I could enjoy the same. Thus, I intended to make the most of the time during those summer vacations. However, my carefree days only lasted for about ten to fifteen days. After that brief period, my mother suggested that I join an English-speaking course advertised on the local channel.

"Khup paise alet na tumchakade?" (You have a lot of money!) I yelled at my mother when she suggested that I join an English-speaking class. Despite knowing that my parents wanted to provide the best education for their child, I was skeptical.

Being a bit more studious than my siblings, my parents were willing to stretch their finances when it came to my education. They aimed to ensure that I never felt limited by their financial capabilities, especially when it came to learning. Consequently, they were willing to make sacrifices to provide the best possible education for me.

Reluctantly, at my mother's insistence, I joined the English-speaking class that summer. The class was predominantly attended by students from Hindi families. My schedule involved two hours of class in the morning from 8 am to 10 am, leaving the rest of the day for full enjoyment. I embraced the summer to the fullest extent, with the exception of those two hours spent in the English-speaking class.

However, my perception of the class quickly changed, possibly within a week of joining. The reason was the overwhelming number of students from Hindi families, especially girls. The class was filled with good-looking girls from Hindi families.

This time, it wasn't about being flashy among the girls; I took the class seriously because I wanted to interact with them. Before joining the class, I could understand English when spoken but had difficulty speaking it, particularly in a grammatically correct manner.

Regular attendance improved not only my English language skills but also my relationship with the teacher. As mentioned earlier, this teacher became a lifelong mentor. He was a kind and gentle person, and over time, our relationship developed into a familial bond.

There have been a couple of incidents in my professional life, which I will share later in the second volume of the book, where I truly thanked this guy from the bottom of my heart. He played a pivotal role in various stages of my life since we first met. Even after almost twelve years, whenever I find time, I make sure to go to the class and meet this gentleman.

However, he is not the only person I had for my life from this class; there are two more whom I can't forget until I breathe my last. One is a boy, now one of my closest friends, rather a brother now than a friend, and the other a girl who could have been my _____, if everything had gone well.

Yes, I am leaving that space blank because those reading this might easily understand what I meant.

This time, unlike always, I am not smiling but a bit emotional, but not regretful. Anyways, that's how life is—things don't go the way you plan them, and when they don't go the way you want, you get angry and annoyed with the almighty. That was my situation in the year 2005-2006 when I was lost in the wilderness, feeling down and out, and utterly alone.

Again, thanks to the Almighty, but before Him, my mother stood by me, as she always does. This was the period when I learned one thing prominently: don't show your weaknesses, or you will be ruined and left with nowhere to turn. People are there to make use of you.

No matter what troubles you have or what problems you are going through, just keep yourself composed and move on. People around you may portray themselves as supportive, caring, kind, and sympathetic, but many will use you if you let them. Of course, there are a few who genuinely care about you, but they are very few.

They say, "GOD has to be seen in a man," right? But how many of those are left today? Very few, hard to identify and understand, and even more difficult to experience.

So, as I said, one thing I predominantly learned here is that if you have to bow down, show your weakness, express your plight, or even cry loudly, please do it before Almighty God, because He will never take advantage of you after knowing your condition. Some may question, "Parents are there, better-half is there." Yes, you are right, but if you do so, they will surely support you, albeit unknowingly making them weak.

Just a couple of lines from the legend Charlie Chaplin:

"Nothing is eternal in this world, not even our problems."

"I like to walk in the rain because no one can see my tears."

So, read them when you are alone, down, and lost. Shake your head, get up, and move on.

Anyways, as of now, we have deviated a lot from the caption; we will come back to this episode of my life later.

As I, along with my entire family, was waiting for the Board examination results, the day finally arrived when the results were out. I can still recall that day vividly. I scored fairly well, and the entire family, including me, was happy. However, I could see in my father's eyes, who never imposed anything on all three of us, be it studies or careers, that he was expecting me to score more than I did.

He never wanted me to buckle under the pressure of his expectations, but I was no longer a kid. I could easily understand, though he never explicitly talked to us about scoring marks and all. Thus, the entire family was happy for me, doing well in the examination.

Frankly speaking, I was missing something and feeling a bit low because I could not meet the expectations of my father. He wanted me to stand in the merit list, not knowing that, though good at studies, I was never a merit student at all. I would have never put in the hard effort to stand in the merit list because I never gave importance to that, and even today, I don't.

The World Is Such A Small Place— It's A 'Small World'

Good Morning.

It's January 27th, 2011, a bright, sunny, pleasant morning, and I am traveling to Delhi.

Yesterday, on January 26th, 2011, I experienced a surprise that was out of this world, proving that the world is indeed a small place— yes, 'It's a Small World.'

To provide you with the details, while hanging out with a few friends late in the evening on the 26th of January, one of my friends was eager to show something on Facebook. He was particularly interested in showcasing pictures from his recent Goa trip. However, none of us were really interested in seeing what he was showing.

One of us jokingly remarked, *"Abe Rakh be tera phone jeb me... hame nahi dekhna."* (Keep your phone in your pocket... we are not interested)

He immediately complied, but I could sense a bit of nervousness in him. He wanted to share his experiences, the fun, and the adventurous activities from the trip. Without wasting a moment, I called out to him, saying, *"Bhai dikha to muje... mai kabhi Goa nahi Gaya."* (Brother, show me; I haven't been to Goa yet)

He gave me a mild smile, aware that I was asking not out of genuine interest but to keep his heart. Still, he played along, pretending I was genuinely interested. Reflecting on that moment, I appreciated the essence of friendship.

He rushed to me and started sharing photos, videos, and recounting the moments from his Goa trip. With equal enthusiasm, I engaged in what he was sharing. To show more interest, I took his mobile and delved deeper into his Facebook profile—friends, photos, and more. That's when I stumbled upon something unexpected.

Can you make a guess? Well, I'll spill the beans.

I found a girl who resembled childhood crush (yes, my childhood crush) among his friends on Facebook. Initially, I was a bit confused, questioning if she was the same girl. To clear my doubt, I delved into the details, only to realize, as I mentioned earlier, that the world is indeed a small place—yes, 'It's a Small World.' She was the same girl.

I didn't know why, but I looked up at the sky and smiled at the Almighty, thinking about how great, infinite, and hard to understand He is. I asked my friend who she was and how he knew her.

"She was with me in college; we studied in the same college," he replied.

It didn't take long for me to recall an incident when he mentioned that she was in the same college where he had studied. It was around the year 2000, perhaps in December or January. I was waiting for the city bus to my college, but as it was getting late, I took an auto-rickshaw to the main bus station.

After boarding the auto-rickshaw and moving some distance, a girl waved her hand towards the same auto-rickshaw, and as it stopped, she boarded. I was once again in a dilemma, wondering if she was the childhood crush. Two reasons fueled my uncertainty: she bore a striking resemblance to the childhood crush, and she boarded from the area near our school.

With some courage, I asked if she was the same girl, and she, with a confirming smile, acknowledged that she was. We chatted for another five to ten minutes before she disembarked at her stop. Essentially, this was the first time I had met her since I left school in 1995.

After this auto-rickshaw encounter in the year 2000, I never met her again, nor saw her photos. We were not in contact at all. Why would she be? The feelings were mine alone, and she was completely unaware of this fact.

Almost ten years later, I saw her photo in my friend's Facebook friend-list.

"Hey, what happened? Where are you lost? What are you thinking? Do you know her?" asked my friend.

"No no", I replied with a lost voice.

"Let's go home, we have had a lot of fun," yelled the boys.

"Yes, I have to go to Delhi tomorrow," I said.

And we dispersed.

However, I was still not out of that Facebook episode. What I had seen was a happy face of the childhood crush, all content with her married life, settled far away from India, in a foreign country. It gave me a kind of joy that I can't narrate, seeing a girl who used to play with me when we were children, having gone that far, happily married and settled. I was genuinely happy for her. One might think that my heart might have been broken, seeing her married, but trust me, there was nothing like that, as I had not followed her for so many years.

However, I don't know why; I thanked God and felt happy that night as I was about to go to bed.

"Arey zopayach nahi ka... khup khush distoy... kay lottery vagere lagli ki kay? Udya Delhi jayach na tula?" (Are you not sleeping... looking very happy... have you won a lottery? you have to go to Delhi tomorrow!), yelled my mother.

"Nahi nahi, jatoy zopayala," (No, no, I am going to bed) I replied.

The next morning, I woke up with the same zeal, but I had a plan in mind. I logged into my Facebook account and sent a friend request to the childhood crush, with no intentions but to be a friend forever thereafter, never to part again. I started waiting to see if she would accept it or not.

Did she accept it? Did we reconnect after almost fifteen years? Did she know me? What if she accepted my request? Did we chat?

Wait, all your questions will be answered when I come to this phase of my life. But for now, I have to catch my Delhi flight. So, bye for now. I am all smiling and happy.

The End Of An Era And Entry Into A New World

You might be a bit surprised to read the caption; hold on, by this, I am referring to that phase of a person where he has to think of his career, his aims, goals, and all. Till this time, I was never too serious about my career; our family background was such that no one except my mother would talk too much about the career and all. So, I would take each day as it came, enjoy it, and live life happily without much future thinking.

But as I passed my tenth board examination, everyone around me got a bit serious about my studies. All of a sudden, people started talking about my future plans, my career, my aspirations, and all that. But to me, I was totally confused.

In that helter-skelter, I somehow opted for the science stream for my future studies at the same school where I passed my tenth grade. Now my world had totally changed. A boy who would enjoy playing with his siblings and friends, accompanying his mother to market, attending functions, chilling with his father, and having the same routine as the other members of the family was suddenly seeing a dramatic change.

I was being given special treatment by my entire family; they would not engage me in any housework, no functions, no play, no movies, no TV. Everyone expected me to study around the clock. Being the eldest son and the eldest of all the brothers, everyone had special expectations of me. Everyone wanted me to do my best in my studies, specifically in higher secondary board examinations. But I was not at all enjoying this; rather, I was getting buckled under the pressure of expectations everyone had from me. I had no choice but to live up to their expectations.

Yes, I wanted to help my father by being the second earner in the family. I wanted to help my mother by doing well in examinations and thus securing the future. I wanted to make my parents and elders proud by excelling in my career. I myself wanted to do something in life to come out of the economic condition we were in, but not at the cost of those days that were never to come back in my life. I was missing that enjoyment, that joy, which I had until that time, and I was even more hurt knowing this time would never come back again. But this is how life goes. You can't expect everything to go the way you want.

Thus, I started studying for my higher secondary school.

My daily routine became monotonous; I would wake up early in the morning, go through my morning routine, have breakfast, attend tuition, return home, head to college, come back, attend tuition again, return home after tuition, have dinner, study until 10 pm, and then go to bed. Quite repetitive, isn't it?

Eventually, I successfully passed the higher secondary board examination with good marks. Feeling a bit lost about my future path, I joined the group of individuals who were uncertain about their next steps. I roamed with one of my college friends, visiting different colleges, gathering information, talking to people, and trying to figure out what to do next. Two options lingered in my mind, without a clear understanding of why or how: one was engineering, and the other was pursuing a science degree. Eventually, I chose engineering.

With the marks I had scored in the higher secondary board examination, I could have easily secured admission to study metallurgy engineering at the regional college in Nagpur. However, due to a lack of knowledge, possibly stemming from not having a strong educational background, I opted for mechanical engineering at a different college.

Choosing this path wasn't without challenges. The foremost concern was whether my father would be able to afford the cost of this four-year professional course, in addition to covering the educational expenses of my siblings. Although I secured a free seat, the annual fees amounted to Rs. 14,000 per year, which, despite being manageable, posed a financial strain on my father. Nonetheless, he managed to arrange the funds.

In the year 2000, I was admitted to the engineering college, marking the beginning of the journey to carve out a meaningful identity in life.

Part- II

I know you have a lot of unanswered questions.

- Why was I attending the office on August 15th ?
- Was I really doing justice to my job, writing this book while on the job?
- Why would I travel to Delhi frequently?
- Why was I sick rather than nervous on September 24, 2010?
- What about the pending Facebook request to the childhood crush? Did she accept it?
- Did we chat? If yes, did I convey to her that I would like her in childhood?
- Did I ever meet childhood crush, who was residing abroad?
- Did I complete my engineering?.........Of course, at some places in this book I talked of taking over the shift from the previous Engineer implies I did......but still.....Did I complete my engineering smoothly?
- Did I ever meet any of the characters, I portrayed, from my school till seventh grade after leaving the school?
- How were the days in engineering, if I did complete it?
- Was there any other girl in my life after the childhood crush?
- What were those incidents in professional life where I truly thanked the English Speaking class teacher?
- What connection did I have with the Center Boy?

And many more. Wait, all these questions will be answered in Volume II.

You Write. We Publish.

To publish your own book, contact us.
We publish poetry collections, short story collections, novellas and novels.

contact@thewriteorder.com

Instagram- thewriteorder

www.facebook.com/thewriteorder

www.ingramcontent.com/pod-product-compliance
Lightning Source LLC
LaVergne TN
LVHW041612070526
838199LV00052B/3112